067766

DATE			

BURT
REYNOLDS

BURT REYNOLDS

An Unauthorized Biography

Sylvia Safran Resnick

ST. MARTIN'S PRESS
New York

A section of photographs follows page 72.

Design by Dennis J. Grastorf

Library of Congress Cataloging in Publication Data

Resnick, Sylvia.
  Burt Reynolds: an unauthorized biography.

  1. Reynolds, Burt. 2. Actors—United States—
Biography. I. Title.
PN2287.R447R47   1983   791.43'028'0924 [B] 82-17075
ISBN 0-312-10876-1

FIRST EDITION
10 9 8 7 6 5 4 3 2 1

With love and kisses
to Max,
The Burt Reynolds in my *life*

Introduction

HIS FIRST PICTURE, *Angel Baby,* released in 1960, paid him $15,000. By the fall of 1978, columnist Rona Barrett proclaimed Burt Reynolds to be the highest-grossing film star ever. To that date, his movies had grossed $4,000,000, and they have gone on to gross over $300,000,000. As many as four of his pictures were being shown simultaneously across the country, and the movie section of *The Los Angeles Times* listed three of those films as playing in the city during just one week.

In the year it was released, 1977, Burt's first good ol' boy movie, *Smokey and the Bandit,* was said to have tied with *Star Wars* as the top money-making film. It still brings in money from rentals.

Burt is considered a super superstar by those who pay the price of admission, waiting patiently in line for a Burt Reynolds movie. But many critics do not recognize him as an "actor" and continue to pan his films and his talent. He continues to strive for critical recognition even though he is a legend in his own time. On a scale of 1–10 in popularity, he is well over the limit, weighing in at at least a 12.

"I just love him. I see everything he's in because he always plays Burt Reynolds," an ardent female fan exclaimed.

"I like his pictures because they're fun and he's so natural," her male companion added.

Who is Burt Reynolds? What makes him turn out film after film in what is considered the fastest, hardest clip an actor has ever run? In a span of ten years he has completed twenty-five films. It would seem to many that Burt is running a marathon race with himself.

What is the reason behind this driving ambition? One might conclude that the seed of ambition was planted during his early years.

BURT
REYNOLDS

CHAPTER ONE

Burt Reynolds was born on February 11, 1936, in Waycross, Georgia, where his father and mother had met and settled after their marriage. Mr. and Mrs. Burton Reynolds named their second child, their only son, Burton Leon. But rather than tag him with the title of Junior for life, they called him Buddy, or Buddy Lee.

A sturdy child with a full, cherubic face and deep-set dark eyes that looked out on the world around him with quiet intensity, young Buddy grew up fighting a constant battle with himself—a battle that all too often erupted outwardly, causing him endless trouble. Those formative years are best described as filled with turmoil and unrest. Learning to understand and accept who he really was at the core of his being was a continuing struggle for Burt that lasted into his adult years. Much of this inner conflict can probably be traced to the turbulent relationship between father and son.

It was not until he had to face a personal crisis later in his life that Burt Jr. came to really know the man he wanted so desperately to reach as a child. In recent years Mr. Reynolds and his famous son have grown very close. The relationship is one of warmth and tenderness, as each man has come to understand the other. But when he was growing up, Burt feared his father, and as a result rebelled against the strict rules Mr. Reynolds imposed upon him.

Burton Reynolds, Sr., was born and raised on an Indian reservation in North Carolina. His mother, Burt's grandmother, was a full-blooded Cherokee who had fallen in love with and married a forestry teacher assigned to the reservation. As soon as he was old enough, Burton Sr. went off to Utah to seek a life as a cowboy.

There he became interested in law enforcement and eventually moved on to Georgia, where he studied to become a police

1

officer. It was while living in Waycross that Burton Sr. met and married an attractive Italian woman. A quiet person, who deferred to her husband in all matters, Fern Reynolds is described by her son as gentle and brave, with the spirit of the early pioneers.

"Once boiling grease spilled all over her back and down her arm. She just walked over to my father and told him to take her to the hospital. She didn't cry, not even a whimper even while the doctors were peeling off her skin," Burt remembers.

The Reynolds' marriage is treasured by their son, who speaks with a kind of awe of the love his parents share. "They love each other so much it's scary. It's one of those real and wonderful marriages that works. One that I have always felt is possible to have."

Mrs. Reynolds remembers Burt as a fine boy, but with a temper. "Sometimes he'd get too big for his britches and his daddy would have to straighten him out. A little straightenin' out and Buddy was a good boy again."

The sting of his father's strap as he went about the task of "straightenin' " him out was familiar to young Burt, who rebelled against the stern rules laid down by his disciplinarian father. "My dad was tough as granite," he recalls.

Burt was ten when his family—mom, dad, and older sister, Nancy Ann—moved to Riviera Beach, Florida, a small community outside West Palm Beach where Burt's father was the chief of police. It was here that rebellion exploded in full force, creating a kind of dual life for the restless youth. At home he toed the line and held to the rules set down by his father, but outside, away from the watchful presence of this man whom he remembers as "an enormous figure who filled doorways," Burt was a bit of a hellion. There was a streak of recklessness that often got him into trouble, for which his father had no tolerance. As the son of the chief of police Burt was expected to set an example, to behave in a manner that would not bring shame or disgrace to the family. There was no room for even the slightest infraction. And so the rift grew between father and son.

"I can't remember ever talking with my father. I was proud of him. He was a brave man and very respected in our community. I respected him but I never felt a real love for him then because I didn't know him. I just tried to be a good kid at home because I was afraid of him. I didn't want him to hit me." Corporal punishment was dealt out as often as Burton Sr. thought necessary.

Burt's earliest memories are tied in with the pale green, small wood-frame house on 37th Street in Riviera Beach. The Reynolds' home was in a lower-middle-income housing development in a neighborhood occupied mostly by fishermen.

"It was a town of really tough families. Most of the kids quit school to work on the fishing boats. We all tried to look as mean as we could." Every morning he went to school wearing his T-shirt sleeves rolled up over his shoulders, his dark hair thickly slicked back with vaseline.

He was taunted by the other boys. "Greaseball" and "Mullet" were derisive labels for the boy who was part Indian, part Italian, living in a fisherman's neighborhood. Burt despised the names.

Of his temper his mother has said, "He'd take just so much and then he'd blow up." The blowups were always aimed at the biggest, toughest boy in the crowd. Some deep, compelling need drove young Buddy to prove his worth with his fists. And yet he knew that there was another side to his nature, one he had to hide for a while.

"I knew that somewhere inside of me was a poet. Maybe not a very good one, but there was another person nobody was ever going to see unless he escaped somehow. I didn't know then that I would be an actor. I just knew that I had to squeeze that other person out of me, like toothpaste out of a tube.

"My whole family was undemonstrative. We never touched each other or expressed our affection openly. Men never hugged each other. And you only cried when someone died. If you cried when you got hurt you were a sissy."

A boy's image of his father, the dominant male figure in his life, looms large. Mr. Reynolds towered over everyone else. He was a man so fearless that he once walked right up to a man pointing a gun at him in a local bar and calmly took the gun away while everyone else scrambled for cover.

Struggling to stifle the other side of his nature, the tender, compassionate, loving side, made it almost impossible for Burt to come to terms with himself until much later in his life. Once, while reading a passage in a book that was very moving, tears began to gather in his eyes and he quickly slammed the book shut and put it away.

A man did not cry.

This emotional ambivalence was what drove him to seek trouble. A junior high school caper, a harmless bit of mischief, resulted in Burt's being made to spend the night in jail by the chief of police, his father. There were no favors awarded him because of Mr. Reynolds' position in the community.

"I was pretty wild. I always got home when my father told me to. But I managed to drive the car eighty-five miles an hour between the house and the grocery store, three blocks away. Being my own man for fifteen minutes was important." It was one way of thumbing his nose at the rules—and at his father. He longed to know and love this man, but winning his admiration and attention was another thing. One day Burt made a big mistake, one he has never forgotten.

The family was at home. Burt was still seething from an afternoon of dodging fists after another dare, the echoes of *Mullet* still ringing in his ears. When his mother said something to him, Burt, without thinking, muttered, "Shut up." Suddenly the room went black.

"When I came to, I was lying in the closet. My father had knocked me right through the door. It was lying on the floor, off its hinges, with clothes strewn all over it."

Standing over him with a stricken look on her face, his mother cried out, "He's dead. I'm telling you he's dead."

"He's not dead," Mr. Reynolds replied. "He's just asleep. When I hit them, they go to sleep."

Burt insists that what his father did that day was justified. "My mother is the last woman in the world anyone should ever say 'shut up' to, especially a smart-mouthed kid."

The world of movies became his haven. It was a place where a young boy's imagination could be captured by bigger-than-life heroes marching across the screen in such films as *Jim Thorpe—All American* and *The Spirit of West Point*. By the time he was in junior high school, Burt was well aware of the fact that there were other people out there, that somewhere outside of his one-dimensional, often chaotic existence other people

4

were laughing and living a far different life than the one he knew in Riviera Beach.

He saw them on the screen, those magnificent football heroes leading their teams to victory, the crowds cheering wildly for them. Burt could almost taste the excitement of those glorious moments.

"I would spend entire weekends at the movies starting at twelve-forty-five in the afternoon. I'd see three movies a day and get out by eleven at night. Movies were an incredibly important part of my life."

He was the stalwart athlete running swiftly to victory, and the debonair ladies' man (Cary Grant was his idol) charming everyone. In the movie theaters Burt could forget the whirlpool of turbulence within him, the frustration and anger that drove him to wreck cars, brawl in the streets, and run away from home.

At fifteen, a runaway episode took him to South Carolina. He wandered around for a while, and one day was arrested for vagrancy. His sentence was to serve as water boy on a chain gang. After a week, the authorities sent him back to Riviera Beach. Ashamed and uncertain as to how he would be greeted at home, Burt decided to bunk at a friend's until he could see which way the wind would blow—whether his father would be hot or cold about the latest mischief. Nothing happened. Mr. Reynolds indicated only the slightest acknowledgment of his son's return. For a year they lived in the same town and passed each other on the street, where Burt's father greeted him coolly. Neither of them gave a sign of anything unusual having taken place. In time Burt returned to the family home, having tried in vain to prove something to his father. It was as though he had never gone away.

A few years before, at the age of twelve, Burt "adopted" Jimmy, a homeless boy a year older than himself, whom Burt brought home from school one day with the announcement, "He's gonna be my brother." The Reynoldses quietly took the boy into their home and hearts.

But nothing really changed. The boys at Central Junior High in West Palm Beach, in their letterman sweaters and clean white buckskins, still tormented Burt in the lunch room, tossing sandwiches at him and daring him to fight. Burt remembers feeling at times as though it were all one big play and everyone around him was acting. If only it had been, if only he could have fulfilled his fantasy to stop the play and say, "Hold it. Let's start over again. I don't like my part. I'd rather be that guy over there."

In time he got his chance to do just that. Quite by accident, Burt found a way to be accepted by his classmates, and from that time on, things became a lot easier.

"We ran a race in gym class one day and I outran everyone. The next day a couple of guys wearing sweaters with big C's came over to me. They'd never talked to me before."

The same boys who had provoked him into lashing out, who had called him "Mullet," now approached him in a friendly manner with a challenge that would open doors that had been solidly closed until then.

They wanted him to race a boy named Vernon Rollison. He was the fastest runner in school. True to form, Burt accepted the dare. Why not? It would be easier than fighting, he hoped.

The moment arrived. Burt and his two new "buddies" walked down the football field. Vernon Rollison was waiting. There was a lot of noise behind them and when Burt turned around, he saw that the entire student body was following them. His heart began to pound. What had he gotten himself into this time? If he lost, he would be even worse off than before. But he *could* win. His features set, a look of determination on his broad face as he reached the goalpost, he removed his shoes and waited for the signal to start the race.

"We ran, and I won. The next day when I got off the school bus everything was different."

He was the new school hero. No longer "Mullet" or "Greaseball," but Buddy to everyone.

"That's when something inside of me went click and I thought, *Aha, this is what it's all about.*" Just run a hundred-yard dash and beat out the best racer in the school and everything is suddenly great, he thought, though at the same time, he worried that someday there would be a race he couldn't win. But there were no other challengers, and Burt was acclaimed the best runner at Central.

He had found a way to release that other person inside him. And it felt wonderful!

"I knew that to be *someone,* you had to have leverage, so I set out to be a really good athlete. If I could outrun everybody, then somebody would listen to me."

And getting someone to listen to him, to see and hear the real Burt Reynolds, has been a life's ambition that he has carefully nurtured to fruition.

CHAPTER TWO

"In my early years I had two emotions," Burt remembers. "Mad and madder. I had the reputation of being a guy you didn't mess around with or else!"

But in his high school freshman year the brawls were somewhat fewer. As a star football player he was accepted, and the need to lash out with his fists was no longer important. He had learned in junior high what being accepted could mean. After he had gained the admiration of his once taunting classmates, Burt realized that he'd won more than a race. Suddenly he was *someone.* He was no longer on the fringe of action but at the center. He basked contentedly in the glow of approval, listening happily to the cheers that followed him on the football field as he displayed his athletic prowess.

The lack of confidence that had festered inside him abated. Exhilarated, propelled by the momentum of his new-found fame, he worked hard to continue scoring winning points, fearful that if he let down, all the glory would disappear. "I went out for football, basketball, baseball, and track."

But there was one area where his lack of confidence continued to plague him. Girls!

He would watch enviously as other boys talked easily with the pretty girls in school. One, a star football player a couple of years older than Burt, became his secret idol. Burt marveled at this boy's ability to stroll casually down the corridor with his arm around a girl.

"The thought of actually holding a girl in public was very painful for me. I was so shy. And the first time I ever put my arm around a girl it felt like a log."

The gates of pleasure opened to him when he was fourteen, a time he looks back on with nostalgia. "I was fourteen and she was forty-two. She was a very wealthy lady, in Palm Beach where I grew up. I used to go in to her store and look around. She was always very nice to me. Then one day it just happened. I wasn't scared, I was ready. When you are fourteen, you are just about as horny as you can be. You don't need knowledge as much as an instinct that takes over.

"She was an attractive, warm, sweet lady plus the fact that she was very sensuous and she dug fourteen-year-old boys. She taught me a lot in that year and she gave me a lot of presents."

Burt kept in touch with her for many years afterwards. "I think of her as a good friend, one I remember with great fondness," he later admitted.

"Years later George Hamilton and I were talking about our first lay and it turned out that he was with her in Palm Beach too." It was an intriguing coincidence that makes him smile at the memory of that crossroad in his life.

Afterwards, it was far less painful to pursue a relationship with a girl his own age. He remembers Mary Alice, who became his sophomore sweetheart. "She was terrific. A great chick and very wealthy. I never talked about the facts of life with anyone, but I don't remember having to teach Mary Alice anything. She was just intuitive."

When Merv Griffin did a pilot for a show entitled "Take Me Home Again," Burt Reynolds was his first subject. One of the people Burt insisted that Merv interview for insight into his young manhood was Mary Alice. Her frank words on how Buddy Lee (Burt's name back then) took her virginity and many other colorful descriptions of their relationship made the interview impossible to use on television, but Burt still enjoyed the incident.

He was making progress. Although some of the rich girls he dated in high school made him call for them at the side door, there was one girl who did much to help Burt get over his insecurities.

"I was in love with a girl in my junior year. She was funny, so many light-years ahead of me in everything. She would come by and pick me up in her car and she made me feel great. I saw rockets when I was with her."

It was the confidence he gained during this relationship that Burt says accounts for his frantic dating during his senior year at Palm Beach High.

"I had morning affairs, evening affairs, switched cars, changed shirts, then raced out to get to the next date. I was terrible, but at the time it was wonderful. That's Youth!"

It was the time of his life. But despite the fame of being a football hero, and running the 100-yard dash from girl to girl, he was still plagued by the reckless, impulsive inner drive that had gotten him into trouble far too often.

"I once got a ticket for driving a hundred and five miles an hour. I completely destroyed three cars. I remember once driving the family car, a Plymouth, and it was raining very hard. I'd driven the car to school and had gone to see a girl afterwards. Later I was driving home in a hurry when it started to pour. I wondered how much the car would slide on the tar road if I jerked the wheel so I tried it and it didn't slide much. I was going sixty-five miles an hour at the time and I wondered what would happen if I gave it a *real* jerk. So I did and the car spun out.

"Well, I was lucky because the door opened and I flew out. I landed on some soft sand by a lake. The car just kept right on going down the road, hit a coconut tree, and the engine landed on the front seat. I was seventeen and hard as nails so I wasn't hurt."

But he worried about his father's reaction. What would happen when his father heard about the incident? Burt shuddered to think of the possible consequences. Arriving home, drenched and shivering from the rain and still shaky from his narrow escape, Burt waited for his father's rage to explode after explaining what had happened. Instead Mr. Reynolds just looked at his son, shaking his head in resignation.

"He acted as if it was just something that this crazy kid of his

9

would do. As if he expected me to do things like that," Burt remembers.

Resilient throughout most of his youth, Burt managed to narrowly escape any serious injury despite his impetuous behavior. And he dreamed of what he thought was the impossible somehow coming true: to go to college.

His family had no money. His father's salary as chief of police in the small town in which they lived couldn't be stretched out enough to pay for tuition. Burt earned his spending money doing odd jobs during summer and after school.

College for him was not even just a fantasy, he told himself; it was simply out of the question.

When his high school football coach told Burt that there was a good chance he could go to college, despite the lack of funds, the young man found it hard to believe.

The world he had glimpsed in the movie theaters was to become a reality for him after all. He had always been confident of his athletic ability. Now he was to be given the opportunity of playing football combined with an education.

He was Jim Thorpe—All American.

"The coach was right. I was offered fourteen football scholarships. To qualify, I had to keep up my sports and catch up on my studies. I did three years of academics in two years."

In September 1954, he went off to Florida State University, where he was described by the Sports Information Office as follows:

Reynolds [Buddy as he was called then] entered Florida State in 1954 weighing 171 pounds and standing 5'9". Ol' number 46 played at the halfback position and was good enough to play on the varsity squad as a freshman.

As a freshman he rushed from halfback position 16 times, for 134 yards and two touchdowns. His average per carry, 8.3, was the second highest on the team that year. He also caught four passes for 76 yards. Burt played a little defense also, intercepting one pass for a seven-yard return.

As far as individual game performances go, Reynolds was a standout in the 1955 Sun Bowl against Texas Western. He rushed seven times for 35 yards and returned one kickoff for 15 yards.

To anyone who understands football, that is quite an impressive record. Impressive enough to earn him two coveted awards: All-Florida and All Southern Conference. More important than the awards, however, was the promise of a contract to play with the Baltimore Colts that was to be Burt's ticket to a bright future. That ticket was to open up a far different future when a twist of fate that nearly cost him his life changed his direction.

But in the fall of 1954 he could not have imagined the events that were to reshape his life. In retrospect he has been heard to say that he has thought a great deal about the part destiny plays in one's life. Undoubtedly he had often pondered the strange twists of fate in his own life, perhaps even wondering at the irony of them.

It was a good life, certainly different from what he had imagined as a youngster trying to hide his hurt at his classmates' name-calling.

At Florida State, he had friends, buddies from the team who were often invited to spend weekends at the Reynolds home in Riviera Beach.

Burt's mother remembers those days well. "The front steps on a Friday night sounded like a herd of cattle was going to charge through the house. Buddy was always bringing home those football players for the weekend." Feeding a bunch of husky young men with enormous appetites didn't bother Mrs. Reynolds. "I loved it," she says.

Burt was big man on campus. Girls flocked around him. But Burt's days of frenetic womanizing were over. By the time he enrolled at Florida State he was ready and eager for a one-to-one relationship. He fell in love.

When they broke up he was hurt and it took a long while for him to come to terms with the fact that the romance had ended. She married a wealthy rancher soon afterwards, and it was about five years later that Burt went to see her and her husband on one of his visits home. He left town feeling free at last of the final remnants of regret over having lost her. Seeing her so happy, Burt too was happy. He has always been very protective of the romantic relationships in his life, always concerned about how the woman was faring even after the final chapter had ended.

11

Like most football players, he sustained some injuries, but not enough to keep him from doing what was expected of him on the field. Then, in his sophomore year, his world was shaken and his life did an abrupt about-face. Out driving one night, he was in a particularly joyous frame of mind. The old impulsive reckless streak came over him and he stepped on the gas, feeling confident that since he was the son of the chief of police, no one would give him a ticket.

But he was wrong. The officer who stopped him on the road was stern and disapproving of Burt's apparent disregard for the law. Feeling somewhat less elated, even ashamed of this latest act of foolhardiness, Burt slowed down to an apologetic thirty-five miles per hour for a while. But once again, Burt grew over-confident as his foot hit the gas pedal and he sped toward home.

Up ahead, seemingly out of nowhere, the glare of headlights came at him. He strained to see what was ahead of him, but it wasn't until he was almost upon it that he realized the vehicle was a truck parked in the middle of the highway. He pressed his foot on the brakes and in a fraction of a second decided what he had to do to save his life. Releasing the wheel, he ducked under the dashboard as the car smashed into the immovable object.

As the men inside the truck raced over to help him, Burt made an error in judgment. "Please call my father. He's chief of police," he mumbled painfully.

The men, who had been loading the truck with stolen goods, jumped into the undamaged vehicle and drove off, leaving Burt to lie bleeding until by good fortune a police car came along on a routine check of the road. The officers searched the crumpled automobile for bodies. They found Burt barely alive, a curled-up mass of blood and broken bones. "I had broken four ribs, punctured my kidneys and spleen, and torn the cartilages in both of my knees."

An operation to remove his spleen was performed. The doctors marveled at this young man whose sheer will seemed to be largely responsible for his staying alive. But it was the end of his football career. The one thing that had kept him going, that had imbued him with some confidence, that had given him the chance to win his father over, was gone.

Following surgery on his knee, Burt spent long days in the hospital slowly regaining his strength. He went home to recuperate some more, and there he experienced the true depths of depression. It engulfed him completely. He was angry and filled with resentment at the dirty trick life had played on him so unexpectedly. The dark depression lay across his heart like an immovable rock.

"The accident wasn't actually my fault and I got a five-thousand-dollar settlement out of it, so I decided to go to New York and kind of bum around for a year."

Leaving his boyhood home and the past behind him, Burt set out for the big city, hoping to lose himself in the anonymity of New York. In the back of his mind he felt that somehow he would find a replacement for the dream that had been shattered by a moment of irresponsibility.

"When I was out there making touchdowns, being a football hero, I was on top of the world. But I had always felt that fear that without my football status I wouldn't be liked." In Burt's mind, the accident had made that nebulous fear a stark reality.

"I lived in the Village in New York and fell into a company of actors. I was depressed and unhappy. I was drinking and well on my way to becoming a bum," he recalls.

His new friends intrigued him, however. He listened with a kind of curious detachment to the discussion of auditions, tryouts, rehearsals, disappointments, triumphs, and failures of those alien people, such as Rip Torn, with whom Burt struck up a friendship. He admired their courage in the face of disappointments but had no idea that one day he would be one of them.

He was immersed in his own misery, absorbed in feeling sorry for himself. The temper that had diminished somewhat while he was a college football hero flared up again, and he got into fights at the drop of a word.

One day this quick-triggered temper nearly caused him to make a very big mistake.

CHAPTER THREE

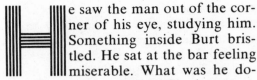

e saw the man out of the corner of his eye, studying him. Something inside Burt bristled. He sat at the bar feeling miserable. What was he doing with his life? For months he had just drifted. The insurance money was nearly gone and the jobs he'd taken to supplement his dwindling funds were dull and meaningless. In his mind he could hear the faint echoes of a cheering crowd. He felt again the rush of excitement that always coursed through him when he raced to glory across the football field. Gone. It was all lost to him. And what was that guy watching him for anyway? Burt tensed, ready for the fight that seemed to be inevitable.

The stranger approached him pleasantly.

"Can you read?"

What the hell was that supposed to mean, Burt wondered, glaring at the intruder. His fists clenched. Looking back, Burt remembers that he was ready to slug him. Instead, Burt heard the man out. Those few moments of conversation with a total stranger set in motion a tremendous change in his life.

"The man was Conrad Hopkins," Burt explains. "What he wanted to know was could I read lines."

Hopkins had once been the secretary of writer James T. Farrell. He had gone on to become a writer himself, one whose work is respected and admired among his peers. He was impressed by Burt, and his rugged, brooding good looks. He was struck by the intensity of emotion that showed in his face. There was something about the young man that compelled Hopkins to suggest that Burt think seriously about an acting career. Later, Hopkins was to encourage the unhappy youth to read the classics, to become familiar with good literature, and to study the contemporary playwrights should he one day decide to pursue an acting career.

Instead, Burt opted to go back to school to wait until his knee healed completely and he could return to FSU and his place on the team. At Palm Beach Junior College, Burt hoped to earn the credits to enable him to get back into FSU when he was ready.

"When I was at Palm Beach J.C.," he recalls now, "it was during a very low point in my life. I felt that I had failed. All of my dreams were shattered. I had nowhere to go with my life unless I could get back to being a football star again.

"There was a certain table in the student center [at Palm Beach J.C.] where all the school jocks sat," he says. "The literature and drama students sat at another table. They were the campus actors. They would file in wearing their turtleneck sweaters and sit together, laughing at us. We were jokes to them.

"But they interested me. So I watched them carefully. A lot of Marlon Brandos, Jimmy Deans, and Carroll Bakers. I went to some of the one-act plays at school and I thought to myself, *Hell, I could do that.*"

Feeling confident of his natural ability, Burt was soon amusing his jock buddies with impersonations of Brando (whom he greatly resembled) and Gabby Hayes, among others. His friends' loud laughter was like soothing balm, and he discovered a form of acceptance unlike any he'd experienced before. They weren't laughing at him, but at what he was doing that amused them. Soon the somber, trouble-ready, embittered side of Buddy Reynolds retreated. Once again the toothpaste tube had been squeezed and out popped yet another personality: a funny, satirical young man who could win attention and admiration without a football under his arm.

Burt discovered something else about himself at Palm Beach Junior College. Fate stepped in once again when Burt enrolled in an English literature course. The man who taught the class was to be instrumental in helping Burt discover a way of expressing his pent-up energy and the deep desire to be liked that had compelled him to seek acceptance in athletics. Burt credits Watson B. Duncan with changing him from a mess into an actor.

As the drama coach at the school, the professor was always on the alert for new talent. One day after class he stopped Burt to inquire whether he had ever acted. Burt shook his head, annoyed. Back in New York when he had drunk beer and sat in on the bull sessions with his acting friends in the Village, Burt had shrugged off suggestions that he become one of them. "I'm not an actor," he had insisted.

Now he looked directly at Mr. Duncan and shook his head. What was all this acting stuff anyway? He wanted only to return to the football field.

Mr. Duncan was not to be put off. "I'd like you to come to the tryouts in the auditorium tomorrow between one and three. I want you to read for a part in the next school production."

"You're crazy," Burt retorted. "I'm not interested in being in a play."

But his interest was aroused. Mr. Duncan had already taught Burt an appreciation of fine literature. Burt had decided after just a short time in Duncan's class that he had been missing a great deal by excluding literature from his life. *Paradise Lost* and the lyric poetry of Byron completely captivated him. Now his professor had tapped Burt's interest in another area.

Feeling somewhat foolish yet strangely curious, he went to the auditions the following day, arriving late. Mr. Duncan nodded approvingly as Burt entered.

"He handed me a script and told me to read aloud. I knew nothing about how to read for a play. But I said a few words and Mr. Duncan told me that the part was mine."

And so he had his first taste of acting. Buddy Reynolds was an actor speaking lines written by someone else and making them very much his own. His portrayal of the role made famous by John Garfield in *Outward Bound* was to unlock the front door to a fascinating new life.

"Suddenly I was striding around like a male peacock," he admits, "performing to another kind of audience. But nobody ever called me a showoff. They told me that my performance was good. And I liked it. I felt that maybe it was what I should be doing."

With that in mind he returned to FSU in March 1956, enrolling in the School of Theater, where he took courses in stagecraft, essentials of acting, essentials of directing, and makeup. His new classes went well, but in the back of his mind lay the hope that he could still get back to the gridiron. The time came when he had to face the fact that that might not be possible. Dejected and miserable, he sought the advice of his friend, Carmen Battaglia, with whom he had shared many a team victory.

"Buddy came to me one night and asked me to help him decide what to do," Battaglia recounts. "He wanted to make the team again. He had had this style of running before the accident that was really something else. Weaving and cutting back. It was beautiful to watch."

And impossible to regain.

Battaglia encouraged his friend to forget about football. "Get yourself to New York. Try acting the way you've been saying you'd like to," he advised.

Burt's performance in *Outward Bound* had gained him a great deal of recognition. He won the Florida Drama Award and with it a scholarship to Hyde Park Playhouse in New York. Seconding Battaglia's suggestion, Professor Duncan encouraged Burt to go to New York and "grow up a little."

It was a difficult decision but one that Burt had to make, and once again the rift between father and son widened.

"My father was very upset. I was the first member of our family who had ever gone to college. And then I quit."

In December 1956, Burt left FSU.

He no longer had the enthusiasm to continue his formal education. In despair of his son ever doing anything right, Mr. Reynolds threw up his hands and gave up on Buddy.

In New York, Burt returned to his former Village hangouts. This time he was more than a spectator, more than an onlooker who was merely curious. He was now a part of that inner circle of talent yearning for that one important break in the theater.

"People would like to think that I was an overnight success," he says. "But I spent two years doing theater in the East before I went to Hollywood to try TV and movies in the sixties."

A season of summer stock took him on the road with Linda Darnell for tour in the play *Tea and Sympathy*. Money was not plentiful, and to supplement his income Burt worked on the docks in New York whenever he could. Looking back on those days of struggle, he remembers, "Twenty years ago when I didn't have money for a place to sleep I slept in cars. Once I lived in a cold-water flat. I shared it with another actor. It was a strange little room with lots of cold water, especially in winter. And sometimes the lights didn't work."

It was during his tour with summer stock that Burt first met Joanne Woodward, who was visiting the playhouse where he was performing. She took a liking to the young man whom she recalls as "the nicest person I'd met in a long time," and introduced him to her agent, who promptly signed Burt as a client.

"I think she took an interest in this shy person (me) who was always peering around the curtains. When I first met Joanne I was so shy that I carried my lunch in a paper bag so I could go off somewhere alone at lunchtime. It wasn't my talent that impressed her," he says of that first meeting.

His debut on Broadway is deeply etched in his memory. He played the role of Mannon in the 1956 New York City Center revival of *Mr. Roberts.* The production starred Charlton Heston and John Forsythe. Burt was very impressed and nervous about meeting such luminaries face to face.

During his time at Hyde Park Playhouse Burt had worked to lose his thick Southern accent, and now he was to appear in a play with a stellar cast. Burt could hardly believe his good fortune. But how would he ever bring himself to talk to Charlton Heston?

"I'll never forget when I looked up and there stood 'Moses' in the doorway. I looked at him standing there, enormous in his topcoat. And I thought, 'I'll never be able to call him Chuck.' "

Burt's sense of humor never deserted him, even in moments like this.

"Then I took three steps into the room, tripped, and fell flat on the floor. And that's how I met my first big movie star," he remembers, laughing.

Burt's small part in *Mr. Roberts* made enough of an impression on someone to secure a screen test at Fox for him.

"It was actually a personality test," Burt explains. "But I had no personality then, not at all. Oh maybe I had some, but I was so shy. I had to rehearse with some guy, to practice having a personality for the test."

On the day of the big event, Burt treated himself to an early morning shave at a barber shop on Eighth Avenue. It was the middle of winter and the weather bordered on freezing. "My face got all cut up and the barber kept putting these pieces of toilet paper on the cuts. Then I went out into the cold and by the time I arrived at the studio where I was having my test, there were all of these bits of paper stuck to my face. I went in and said, "Hello. I'm Buddy Reynolds."

In retrospect the story is amusing, but at the time he was bitterly disappointed not to get the job. As he left the studio, he wondered if he would fail in this endeavor as he had in football.

His resemblance to Marlon Brando made it even more difficult for Burt to get a firm toehold as an actor. Time and again it worked against him. Burt's temper worsened with each career frustration. The barroom brawls became more frequent, and he soon earned a reputation for being quick with his fists.

Still he persisted, determined to make it somehow. By then he had had a good taste of the theater and savored it. One way or another he would go on to fulfill Watson Duncan's prophecy. "I know you'll make it, Burt," the professor had said.

He remembered the wonderful waves of love that had engulfed him as he performed on stage the very first time. And it was always the same. No matter how small his part might be, the magic and excitement of the theater was now in his blood. The promise of stardom was there, perhaps tenuous and barely within his grasp. But it was there nevertheless.

One day, he assured himself, it would lie right in the palm of his hand.

CHAPTER FOUR

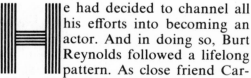e had decided to channel all his efforts into becoming an actor. And in doing so, Burt Reynolds followed a lifelong pattern. As close friend Carmen Battaglia said of him, "Second best wasn't ever good enough for Buddy."

But critical acclaim wasn't paying the bills, not even for the bare necessities of a cold-water flat and a meager diet. When his friend Rip Torn asked if Burt would like to do a stunt job on an upcoming television show, Burt was impressed by the amount of money he would be paid.

It was a simple stunt. All he had to do was pretend to be stabbed and tumble off a cliff. Looking back, Burt says of his introduction to stunt work, "It was the fastest hundred I had ever made."

Afterwards he no longer had to worry about where his next meal was coming from. His stuntman jobs were regular and so was the pay. His sturdy, muscular build and athletic grace served him well as Burt performed his stunt work with a minimum of injury. Falling down stairs or being thrown out of windows covered the bills. But it did not make him an actor, and that was what he wanted to be.

Meanwhile, he continued to study with fine drama coaches, such as Wynn Handman. And whenever he appeared in a play, no matter how small the role, his performance won the approval of critics and audiences alike. He also attracted the attention of talent scouts from Hollywood, and eventually Burt headed for the West Coast. Armed with an envelope filled with reviews extolling his talent, Burt Reynolds arrived in Hollywood in January 1959. He had signed a seven-year television contract with MCA-Universal Studios.

At MCA there was a feeling that Reynolds had something special. "MCA president Lew Wasserman had brought me out from New York. He told people that I was going to be a big star. At MCA when Lew Wasserman says it's going to rain, everybody puts up an umbrella," Burt says.

But it would take the right person to channel Burt's unique quality properly. His trigger-fast temper, rotten and terrible by his own description, was to create a very personal monster, one that very nearly cost Burt the acting career he wanted so much.

At Universal, Burt reported for work in a new series, "Riverboat," which starred Darren McGavin. "I was a green kid as far as working in films was concerned," he says of his role as the young riverboat pilot, Ben Frazer. "Instead of helping me, McGavin looked on me with contempt. He did everything but destroy me on camera."

What the star of the series actually did, Burt related in a 1963 interview, was sabotage his performance every time he was about to step in front of the camera. "We'd run through a scene a couple of times and then just before the camera rolled, McGavin would say to me, 'You're not going to play it *that* way, are you?' What little confidence I had would go right down the drain."

He grew angry. Concerned about what might happen if his temper exploded on the set, Burt gave vent to it in another way. "I'd drive down to Skid Row and walk into a bar. Then I'd wait for someone to make the inevitable crack, belt the guy in the teeth, and go home feeling much better."

Despite the fact that he had hoped that "Riverboat" would be his big break into show business, Burt wanted out of the series. He is said to have gotten so angry in one incident during the filming that he threw an assistant director into a lake. Word of the undercurrents on the set began to circulate the Universal lot. Whether or not Burt was aware of the rumors became secondary to his strong desire to be released from the show.

"I wasn't doing anything or learning anything about acting," he recalls. "I had lines that went 'Are the Indians going to attack us?' I was nothing but a dum-dum riverboat pilot. None of my close-ups even made it on the air."

But the studio ignored his request to be released from the series. It wasn't until he threatened to "blow up the damned riverboat" that someone decided to contact Burt's agent.

"If he says he'll blow the thing up, let him go because that's exactly what he'll do," said Monique James of MCA.

Burt was released with a lecture on his ingratitude.

The consequences were soon evident. In a short time Burt realized how badly his reputation had suffered. The grapevine runs fast and tenaciously through the back lots of Hollywood. This time it carried the unpleasant news of Burt's lack of cooperation. He was labeled a hothead, an ungrateful young man.

His punishment was soon apparent too. The doors to every major studio in town were closed to him.

Ironically, he was to return to Universal a decade later to film *Smokey and the Bandit,* a movie that has grossed millions, but after one season and twenty-six episodes on a top-rated television series Burt was out in the cold as he had never been before.

"I couldn't get a job. I didn't have a very good reputation," he admits. "I worked in every lousy syndicated show, things like 'Pony Express,' the kind of shows that they shoot with a Kodak and a flashlight. They were depressing years but that's where I finally learned to act."

He also picked up another agent, Dick Clayton. Over the years the friendship between the two men grew strong. Burt is quick to credit Clayton's encouragement and faith in him. His dedication to Burt's career is largely responsible for the ensuing breaks that came Burt's way. Part of the time Burt sought to reestablish himself in the acting world he had been in on Broadway. In a short-lived production in which he gave a sterling performance, *Look: We've Come Through,* he received reviews that made him realize he was not wasting his time. He continued to work as a stuntman, studied his craft, and in 1962 returned to series television again.

As Quint Asper, the half-breed Indian blacksmith on "Gunsmoke," Burt was typecast without the studio being aware that he was part Indian. The role was limited, and dissatisfaction again set in. Would he ever be given a real opportunity to show his true talent, or was he destined to continue playing heavies, brooding Indians, and surly nobodies forever?

The answer Burt hoped for was slow in coming, but from time to time there were glimmers of hope that kept him going. "I tested for 'Long Hot Summer' but Tom Moore at ABC said I wasn't pretty enough for the part," he remembers. Roy Thinnes got the role instead.

He had come to the realization back in New York, during those first months of work with the Hyde Park Playhouse, that his strong resemblance to Marlon Brando was not in his favor. Despite the facts that Brando was lighter in coloring, a few years older, and trimmer (Burt was twenty pounds heavier in those days), Burt was often stopped by autograph seekers who would not believe him when he assured them he was not Brando. Reynolds worked at changing his mannerisms, carefully eliminating any gesture or speech pattern that might resemble Brando's.

One night the inevitable occurred. Burt and a date went to a restaurant in Beverly Hills. A man he recognized as a Hollywood agent rushed over to Burt as he entered the restaurant,

22

and before he knew what was happening Burt was being led to a table. He stopped dead in his tracks at the sight of Brando. There he was, intent upon his conversation with the man seated beside him. The agent gushed on about the marvelous resemblance between Brando and young newcomer Reynolds. To Burt's embarrassment, the star didn't even glance up, but merely stuck out his hand and continued his conversation. The story goes that Burt's temper exploded. Hurt and humiliated, he called Brando names that were not exactly in keeping with the elegance of the restaurant. Then, leaving his date, he turned on his heel and strode out without a backward glance.

Whether Brando reacted to the tirade is not known. Burt drove to Brando's house and waited for him. "I didn't know what I was going to do. I think that I wanted to tell him it wasn't my idea. That I hadn't asked to meet him. But he never came home that night."

Burt described his role of Quint Asper in "Gunsmoke" in much the same way that he might have described himself at the time. "He's a guy who loves physical contact, has no prejudices, is completely independent, takes people at face value, and would just as soon fight as eat."

The fact that his unplanned and very embarrassing meeting with Marlon Brando did not end in a few wild punches astounded even him afterwards.

In spite of the lack of acting challenge, "Gunsmoke" proved to be rewarding. His relationship with the stars of this series was one he considers a positive influence. Milburn Stone, who played Doc, gave him advice that Burt has never forgotten.

"The audience will always forgive you for being wrong and *exciting*. They never forgive you for being right and *dull.*"

"I worked with some nice guys during my early days," Burt said in an interview. "Guys like Jim Arness, Milburn Stone, and Ricardo Montalban."

It was because of the encouragement and kindness of these actors that Burt persisted despite his disappointments and what he considered the rut of typecasting. Norman MacDonnell, producer of "Gunsmoke," once said of him, "I have the feeling that if he ever got the bit in his teeth, he'd run away with it. He's not afraid of man, beast, or God. Yet he's really made an effort to fit in with us. It's not easy for a newcomer to break into a cast that's been working together like a family all these years."

He went on to pay Reynolds a great compliment: "I think he's a good actor. Innately, he's a leading man. That creates a problem for us. We can't use him as a leading man. But we get so many letters saying 'enjoyed the show last night with Matt, Kitty, Doc, and the *blacksmith.*' "

Eventually this faint praise wore thin and Burt left the show after two and a half years. His reason was the same as before— he hated his "nothing" role. Friends, other actors, everyone said he was crazy to give up a steady job.

"I was making fifteen hundred dollars a week. But I thought it was a choice between a lifetime of playing half-breeds and maybe someday playing a part that was funny and a little sweet, vulnerable, and crazy. So I quit."

Being called a dirty half-breed in scenes throughout most of the episodes was just too much.

"I guess I could have stayed on that show for years and made good money, but I didn't want to limit myself anymore."

It was a period of strife, but as difficult as those early years were for Burt there were compensations. Life was not all black. It was a time of forming important, lasting friendships, a time when love and marriage entered his life. And most significantly, there was an emotion-packed reconciliation with his father.

CHAPTER
FIVE

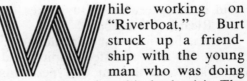

hile working on "Riverboat," Burt struck up a friendship with the young man who was doing the stunts. Hal Needham turned out to be a kindred spirit. The two men quickly learned how much they had in common, and the friendship went on to grow stronger with the years. Both were athletic and very ambitious, and each was somewhat disenchanted about his childhood. Hal too was a Southern boy. Born in Tennessee and raised in Arkansas and Missouri, he recalls the common bond that drew the two young men together: "It's that good-old-boy country kind of people that we come from. We were both trying to get a foot in the door and be *somebody* when we first met."

Although Reynolds had earned his living as a stuntman during the lean years, he was now the second lead on a popular series. Yet he liked to do his own stunts and usually took over when Hal, his stunt double, was supposed to step in.

"What was really funny," Hal explains, "is that back then [1959] they wanted a guy to fall downstairs and still keep talking. A stuntman-actor."

Which was exactly what Burt had become. Doing his own stunts was important, but he had also honed his craft and was a promising actor looking for a real break.

"On 'Riverboat' he didn't give me much chance to double," Hal remembers. "There'd be a fight scene and instead of me fighting, Burt would get in and do it himself. When a jump came he would double his own jump.

"Then one time he mentioned that he didn't know much about motorcycles, so I suggested that he come over to my place and practice. I had motorcycles and a tree where we used to do high falls. Every weekend there were fifteen or twenty stunt guys practicing. Burt started coming around every weekend. He got along well with all of the guys."

It wasn't until years later that Hal learned how close Burt had come to being another kind of star. Modest and always unassuming, Burt never mentioned his brilliance on the football field, just that he had played football in college until his accident. Then one day Hal paid a visit to Burt's house and there they were, the trophies awarded to his friend for a sport he had once made his life's ambition—Player of the Game, All City, All Conference. They told a story without words.

Today Hal believes that Burt's car accident was "a lucky break." His good buddy concurs.

There have been many trials as well as triumphs in the twenty-three years of the Needham-Reynolds friendship. Both have gone through unhappy divorces. Both have persevered to make it big in Hollywood. Hal has stood by at a time when friendship and loyalty were of primary importance in Burt's life. Burt has gone all out to help his good friend realize a long-time ambition.

It was Burt who made it possible for Hal to fulfill his dream of directing a picture. Hoping to convince producer Ray Stark that Hal could be a director, Burt managed to persuade Stark to let Hal direct some test shots. Then, several weeks later, when *Smokey and the Bandit* was being negotiated, Burt asked for his friend to direct.

"It was the biggest thing anyone has ever done for me in my life. Without Burt, I'd never have had a chance," says Hal. "Burt has this capacity for loyalty and caring. He has made it and he doesn't forget anyone he has ever cared for, man or woman."

While Hal and Burt were becoming good friends, another important person came into Burt's life. It was during the tension-ridden season of "Riverboat" that he fell in love. But not at first sight. At least it wasn't that way for the girl.

"In 1960 I met a girl named Judy Carne," he reminisces. "She was the first absolutely free spirit I had ever known. A combination of Tinkerbell, Peter Pan, and Sadie Thompson, all rolled into one. A terribly bright girl who had a real hate for any kind of macho character."

Burt's wild shenanigans—jumping into swimming pools from third-story windows, frequent brawls with anyone who made him angry, as well as his reputation for being a troublemaker on the series—did impress the British actress. The impression was that Burt was a man she did not admire.

"God, you're boring," she commented after one frenetic incident she witnessed.

Judy was a struggling young actress, fresh from England. Her sensibilities were shocked and offended by the actions of this belligerent young man. Yet she sensed something different beneath the surface brawn. There was a special electricity between them. She managed to convince him that it was not necessary to fight his way to success. Eventually, Burt found himself ready to make the important commitment of marriage.

He was twenty-four years old and in love.

But the girl he had chosen to marry was very different from

any of the other girls with whom Burt had been romantically involved. All the others had been generously endowed. Judy Carne was tiny and had a boyishly slim figure. She was cute, a vivacious sprite. There was something about her that caught Burt's eye, and in no time at all, his heart. Perhaps it was her independence of spirit, her ability to make him laugh even at himself, and the fact that Judy knew what Burt hid from most people.

Except for the four years they were together, the sixties could have been almost too grim for him to bear. He was locked into an image on TV: the dull, stoic half-breed who did little more than flex the muscles in his face in most of the television episodes in which he was cast. It was Judy who reawakened the sense of humor that had come to the surface for a little while during Burt's stint as an award-winning actor at Palm Beach Junior College.

They lived together happily before marriage for a year and in 1963 were married in North Hollywood. The bride wore a white gown. The groom wore a joyous smile. Both were very much in love and optimistic about their future together. Burt had taken Judy home to meet his parents, who were immediately won over by her. Life appeared to have taken a turn for the better at last.

For a while they laughed together. That was while love was still fresh and exciting, before career frustrations ate away at the marriage.

"Sometimes the things that attract you in the first place are the things that drive you crazy in a marriage," says Burt.

But Burt's idea of marriage was based on what he knew of the marriage of his own parents. "If you come from the kind of background I do, you think about settling down and having babies."

It didn't work that way with Judy. She was ambitious. Her career was every bit as important to her as Burt's was to him.

"We destroyed one another during our marriage," says Judy. "Burt and I are strong people and our egos were just too big in those days. Neither of us was willing to give."

He wanted her to change, to be a conventional wife. Burt admits that his concept of their marriage was based on a "Fa-

27

ther Knows Best" ideal. Yet he knew that the free-spirited, laughing young woman he had fallen in love with could not change.

His career was floundering. He made two movies for United Artists, *Angel Baby* and *Armored Command*, in 1961, and then went on to play Quint, the half-breed blacksmith in "Gunsmoke." Marriage and career were running neck and neck on the track to disaster. But Burt kept plugging away at both.

Judy recalls: "It was a wild trip, our marriage. The hostility got so out of hand that one day I bought Burt a punching bag."

Burt remembers it this way: "It turned out that I absolutely couldn't deal with her ideas of freedom. I didn't think they were progressive. I thought they were crazy! But the divorce was my fault, my loss. She's a terrific person. We had something special together," he told a reporter during an in-depth interview in the mid-seventies.

During the time of Burt's marriage to Judy Carne, his good buddy, Hal Needham, had also gotten married. The two couples often got together with other married friends. Hal vividly remembers the breakup of Burt's marriage.

"Burt doesn't take relationships lightly. He comes from a great family and he'd expected his marriage to last forever. That divorce really grieved him."

The two separated in 1965. On October 25, 1966, *The Hollywood Reporter* ran an item stating that Judy Carne's divorce from Burt Reynolds had just become final.

Soon after the divorce, Judy Carne was a household word as the "Sock It to Me" girl on the highly popular "Laugh-In" show. Judy's career had finally begun to move forward and as her popularity grew, Burt's diminished.

To make matters worse, Burt had to face his father's bitter disappointment. He had won his dad over during the time of "Gunsmoke." "I had finally gotten on a television show my father could identify with. It was one of his favorite series. And then I quit. It was a little bit the way he felt when I was rejected by the army because of my knee. It was one of the biggest disappointments in my dad's life. He was a real gung-ho Army man."

Then, in 1965, shortly after he and his wife had decided to separate, Burt was on the phone to his mother with still another failure. "Mom, tell Dad he's right about me. I'm just a quitter."

His father did something then that was totally unexpected. He came on the phone and, in a tone that commanded attention, said, "I want you to come home. I'm going to tell you about the things in my life that I've failed at."

Shocked, Burt bought a plane ticket for West Palm Beach. On the long flight, all he could think of was that he was the only one in his family to be divorced. For hours he wrestled with a familiar feeling of inadequacy. He had botched up his career, loused up his marriage. At twenty-nine he had only a string of failures to his credit. How could his father feel anything but shame for his only son?

Mr. Reynolds was waiting at the airport. They rode home in silence. When they arrived, Burt's father did another surprising thing. "He offered me a drink. He had never done that before. We had two shots of cognac. I remember thinking, 'I wish you'd just come right out and say you hate me or you love me or that I've been unforgivable.' "

Instead, Mr. Reynolds began to tell his son about his own mistakes. There was compassion and understanding in his voice as he revealed a side of himself that Burt had never dreamed existed. His father recognized that everyone makes mistakes in life. It was like a miracle. In the midst of his total misery, Burt began to feel a surge of hope.

A torrent of emotions rose to the surface as the son listened in astounded silence to the father. "I cried and my father got tears in his eyes. We began hugging each other and crying. Suddenly he became a different person. A gregarious, humorous, wonderful man who had been hiding behind the facade of a police officer."

Burt was different after their talk. The sadness about the failure of his marriage was still there, and for a long time after they separated and divorced, Judy and Burt would feel that same magic, that tremendous pull of attraction and desire for one another whenever they met. But it was over, and Burt had to accept that fact and go on.

"When I made that phone call, my dad must have sensed that I was really at a crossroads. Failure, like success, is habit-forming. I was so lost and mad. This is a great town to slide in because there are so many people sliding with you. Into dope, alcohol, sex. You can find a whole group that doesn't ever want to surface."

The phone call had been a subconscious cry for help. Something in Burt did not want to slide into the mire of hopelessness, knowing what it would do to him.

"There's an old southern expression that no man is a man until his father tells him he is. There's many a young southern man still getting drunk, still doing crazy things in cars. Still doing that whole macho thing, trying to find some John Wayne figure to tell him he's a man."

For Burt that man was his father.

"Out of that moment with my dad came a strength of character. I became a whole new guy. I wasn't afraid to fail, and if I was going to fail, I was going to fail big. To make it in this business takes luck, guts, and knowing when to throw it into second gear and floor it. I knew after that time with my dad it was going to be that way.

"I was shattered by the divorce so I went to New York. I had decided that if they didn't want me there I'd go anywhere."

But New York welcomed him with the chance to do a series, this time as its star.

CHAPTER SIX

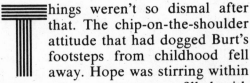hings weren't so dismal after that. The chip-on-the-shoulder attitude that had dogged Burt's footsteps from childhood fell away. Hope was stirring within him again, and he was once more a young man filled with confidence.

Yes, his marriage had failed and his career seemed to have bogged down. But the door to communication, to better understanding between father and son, had opened wide.

"I think my dad learned as much about me as I learned about him that day. No one in our family had ever been in the arts before. Jimmy, my adopted brother, was always an outstanding athlete. He's a high school coach now. My sister,

Nancy Ann, is married and leads a nice, average life. Up until that day my dad just hadn't been able to understand me and my needs.

"Afterwards he was no longer a great shadow who stood in the doorway saying 'don't do this,' or 'do that.' As soon as we finished talking I grabbed him and gave him a great big bear hug. I told him that from that time on whenever I saw him or my mom I would hug the daylights out of them. And that's the way it's been ever since."

So the way was easier. The barriers lifted. Feeling much better about himself and this wonderful new relationship with his family, Burt moved to New York, determined to throw himself into his career. Being an actor meant so much to him: acclaim, travel, money. Acting was the chance to be somebody. This time he felt that he would make it.

Burt went to auditions for "Hawk," a television series about a New York detective, and discovered that they wanted to do a personality test on him. Recalling what had happened once before when he was tested for "Long Hot Summer" and had been turned down because he wasn't pretty enough, Burt was less than enthusiastic about it. But René Valente, the production consultant on the show, said it had to be done. She used a novel approach, however, which proved to be right.

"She climbed up on a ladder so [the camera] could see my eyes. I asked her if Tom Moore would be seeing the test and she said yes.

"Well, I'm not any prettier now than I was before," Burt retorted, certain that he would be turned down for the part.

Instead he received a pleasant surprise. Tom Moore signed him on to star in the ABC series. "He said that I had the quality of anger they wanted for the role," says Burt.

Hawk was portrayed as a hostile young man, and despite the change within him, Burt had not completely shaken the remnants of the resentment and hostility he had carried around for thirty years. Nevertheless, his attitude was much more relaxed and the reputation of being a hothead did not pursue him in his new role.

Hawk was to be the on-screen detective of everyone's imagination. He was described in the studio press release as "a 1966 Model American Indian of Iroquois descent who is attached to the night side of the D.A.'s office." Burt's own Indian heritage was a plus for him in the minds of the studio decision-makers. They saw this virile, good-looking, somewhat impassive actor as the perfect choice for the part.

But Burt was unhappy with the original image scripted for this tough, streetwise cop. He felt it was not an accurate portrayal. Balking at the idea of having Hawk wear knives up his sleeves, Burt decided he had to try to effect some changes. This time it had to be right.

"My idea for the series was a man who didn't talk gibberish or get plastered [the drunken Indian image was appalling to him]. If everybody else had had their way, I'd have been running around in moccasins and feathers with knives up my sleeves."

He explained his concept of Hawk to those in charge, and the character was adapted according to Burt's suggestions. At last he could see a glimmer of light on his career. He was happy with the series and even more pleased with the freedom the studio had given him to interpret the role of Hawk as *he* saw the character.

After directing the final two segments of "Hawk," Burt was eligible for membership in the Directors Guild, an honor he accepted happily when he received his membership card in September 1967, just after completion of *Fade In* for Paramount.

"When I think back to these early days of my career, I see that 'Hawk' was one of the happiest times of my life in the business. For the first time I didn't feel like a chess pawn. I helped direct, cast, and write scripts. And I fought the establishment at every turn."

It was the start of a new era for Burt.

Hal Needham, with whom he had developed a close friendship off screen and a trusted relationship on, had bowed out of his job as stunt double when "Hawk" went into production. Given the opportunity to work as a stunt coordinator on a feature film, he reluctantly remained in Hollywood, so Burt asked another friend, a boxer named Stan Barrett, to step in. Stan was to work with him throughout the shortlived "Hawk," a number of feature films, and the equally shortlived "Dan August" before he was injured in a stunt accident.

During his long tenure with Burt, the agile Barrett was called upon to do only certain types of stunting as the actor continued to do his own stunts, despite occasional mishaps. Stan had developed his stuntman career through the efforts of his friend Burt and he had many good things to say about Reynolds in a 1970 interview.

"I was a boxer, not a stuntman, when we first met. Then one day Burt arranged for us to do a boxing scene. It was great because Burt really made it look good. He is the best friend I ever had. Once when we were doing a show and he was doing his own stunts as usual, someone asked why they needed me. Burt told them that he wouldn't get off the chair unless I was there."

It was the familiar pattern of unwavering loyalty.

"When a guy is needed to fight with Burt I do the fight with him. He's very athletic and in any bind, that ability pulls him through. Physical things trigger him," Stan continued. "Burt needs the stimulus of physical action. It turns him on. It's not ego. He has a tremendous amount of humility. I don't know if I could be like that if I was in his shoes. And his sense of humor is something else.

"Burt is a guy who remembers his friends and looks out for them. And he really dislikes it when anyone is not using their potential."

While he was portraying a man of Indian descent on screen, Burt had quietly become involved with helping the American Indian. He has continued to be active in that cause but has never tooted his own horn nor allowed anyone else to do so. Yet his feelings on the issue run deep.

"I feel very strongly about it. But I don't think that I am a spokesman for the American Indian (as some others profess to be). You can't speak for the American Indian because they have three hundred different languages. And each tribe has its own likes and dislikes about the others. That's why there has been no official spokesman for so many years," he told a reporter while being interviewed on the set of "Dan August." "They don't know how to get one.

"If you care about something you have to devote yourself to it. And you don't do it loud."

After only four episodes had been aired, "Hawk" was abruptly cancelled. The series had failed to show up in the ratings. Despite the quality of the scripts, the excellence of the acting, and all the other elements that go into the making of a good television series, it was zapped into oblivion. The competition had won out.

Burt was crushed with disappointment. He had tried, had really made an all-out effort. Hawk had been real to him. But somehow he had failed to make him real enough for the viewers.

He was proven wrong when, by January 4, 1967, the mail rooms of both *The New York World-Journal Tribune* and the ABC network had received hundreds of letters from viewers angrily protesting the cancellation of "Hawk." The letters insisted that the show was better in every way than most of what was on television at the time, and they praised the caliber of Burt Reynolds' acting. The letters from women viewers were the most emotional.

René Valente commented after going through many of those letters, "What Burt projected was sheer animal sex."

Yet stardom still eluded him. And so began a round of filmmaking that was to take Burt to many distant ports of call as he accepted any and every film offer that came along. Something compelled him to say yes, something that made it very important that he keep his image before the public. As long as an actor does not slide into oblivion, he has a chance. Burt was determined to keep himself before the camera. Fortunately he was in demand for any number of roles, all calling for the macho image he portrayed so well.

In rapid succession he made films such as *Shark, Navajo Joe* in Italy, *Fade In, Impasse, Sam Whiskey, 100 Rifles* in Spain, and, in Jamaica in 1969, another adventure picture, *Skullduggery*.

Producer Saul David had signed Burt to make *Skullduggery* at the prompting of his wife, who could not forget the impact Burt had made upon her as Hawk.

"She kept nagging me about this beautiful, sulky guy. So I took a look at some film from the show and he was just what we wanted."

David went on to state that although *Skullduggery* did not make Burt the big star he should have been at the time, he felt that Burt had missed stardom on a number of occasions by only a slight margin. Saul David's faith in Burt's potential was to be realized in time, but not before more sorrow and disappointment had come Burt's way.

CHAPTER SEVEN

hile the roles he was playing on the big screen were far from earthshaking, Burt was being well paid for his acting efforts.

"My movies," he has often remarked in retrospect, "were the kind they show in airplanes and in prisons because nobody can leave."

Critics were kinder to him then than they would be later in his career. They praised his acting, but those who made the financial decisions within the film industry were oblivious to that praise. Burt chafed, wondering if he would ever rise above the mediocrity of his movies. A remnant of hope remained.

"Someone is going to have to take a chance on me," he sighed.

Whether or not that someone would ever materialize was a constant question, and he often grew impatient for the answer. Burt invested his money. His first purchase was a 180-acre parcel of land in Jupiter, Florida, a small town outside of Palm Beach. On the property was a house built in 1923 by gangster Al Capone, as a hideout for him and his henchmen when the heat in Chicago became unbearable. Fascinated by its history, Burt loved to tell friends and acquaintances the origin of his new home. He spent a great deal of money to remodel it, adding a guest house, a pool, and a gym. And eventually, as his imagination took off, a tree house such as fantasy is made of was built above a grove of pine trees some fifty yards from the main house, overlooking the property.

"The top is like a mushroom," he said, describing the all-glass house reached by a carpeted spiral staircase. "There's a balcony and a swinging bridge leading to a gazebo. A canal runs around the house so it has the appearance of being on an island. There's a tremendous stereo system with nine speakers.

The carpeting runs from the floors right up the wall. It's all double thickness in green and yellow, like a tree."

The tree house is soundproof as well and comes complete with an alligator named Fred, who swims about in the lake that is stocked with bass. Fred loves to eat ice cubes.

A little boy's hiding place is made into a grown man's private retreat, a whimsical expression of the light side of Burt Reynolds—a side only a few were privileged to see in the early years of his career. Nearby, in the main house, his parents reside as managers of the property. A few dogs and cats roam the Ranch (as he and his family refer to it), giving it the feel of a real country home.

In time Burt invested in more land, this time in Arkansas. He formed his own production company with an idea of one day producing his own pictures. It was the way to go in a changing industry. And so the Reynolds financial empire began to take shape. As long as he was making money, Burt had decided to build some security against a time when his acting career might end from lack of recognition. Yet he held onto the hope that someone would offer him the role that would bring him that long-awaited recognition.

An old football injury was giving him considerable discomfort. After the automobile accident, the damage had become aggravated to the point that it was soon evident that surgery would be necessary. In May 1969, Burt entered the hospital for an operation on his knee in the care of the same doctor who had treated Joe Namath. The first night home from the hospital, Burt surprised his friends by showing up at a party. He spent the evening kidding about his operation, amusing everyone with his usual quick wit.

Within three months he was literally back on his feet again and into production on his next film.

Television had been a bitter disappointment. He had really counted on the role in "Hawk" to provide a stepping stone to success. Films were making him wealthy, but there were no rockets going off bearing his name. Burt longed for those rockets. Obscurity was not for him, even if it was safe and secure. He felt at times as though he were standing on a mountain ledge waiting for someone to signal to him which way to step next. One way would take him straight to the very top of the mountain. The other could plunge him headlong into oblivion.

It was only when he was within the close circle of a few really good friends that he was able to let go of the uptight actor image and be himself. Don Meredith, Hal Needham, Stan Barrett, and Glen Wilder comprised this inner circle. With them he was far different from the hard-living, strong and silent, macho man who came across the screen so much larger than life. In the presence of his good buddies, Burt was a warm, friendly, sensitive man whose quick wit was often directed at himself.

Since his divorce, he had approached dating on a nonserious basis. He was satisfied to play the field. But then a beautiful, talented actress named Inger Stevens came into his life. The two met while costarring in an ABC Movie of the Week. In the film, "Run Simon Run," Burt again was portraying an Indian. How the romance began is something only a few intimate friends have ever really known. The relationship was a well-kept secret, even from the ever-present, alert members of the press. Both cherished their privacy, something their careers as actors made almost impossible to attain. It wasn't until shortly after the death of Inger Stevens that the fact of their romance became a widely read item.

On the Monday evening prior to her tragic death, *Variety* reported later, Inger and Burt had dined at La Scala with producer Aaron Spelling and his wife. On Thursday, April 30, 1970, *The Los Angeles Examiner* reported that Inger Stevens had been found unconscious in her Hollywood Hills home that morning by a friend. Her death was later ruled suicide from an overdose of barbiturates.

In the May 13 issue of the *Examiner,* a follow-up feature stated that the actress's roommate had said that Inger planned to marry Burt Reynolds sometime later in the year. It had been Lola McNally, a good friend of Miss Stevens, who had found Inger's body in the kitchen.

Only those few people who were close to Burt knew what he was really feeling. His sorrow was private and privileged, something everyone respected. The fact that he had been in love with Inger Stevens was all that the public was ever told. The subject has remained a delicate one.

Reporters were cautioned by studio press people to avoid any mention of Miss Stevens during interviews with Burt. To date he has not discussed this relationship publicly. "Run Simon Run" was shown on ABC in October 1970. Ironically, Burt was the recipient of the National Cowboy Hall of Fame Wrangler Award for his performance in the television movie.

He was now thirty-five years old. For a dozen years he had been trying to make it in Hollywood, in New York, all over the world. He had given them all a shot but nothing had as yet worked that magic that he felt, deep within him, was still possible. He began to think seriously about returning to television. There were millions of viewers who could become Reynolds fans if only he could find the right vehicle. One afternoon he joked about it with his agent, Dick Clayton, over lunch. He might consider doing another series.

"I'll try it again if it can be with somebody like Quinn Martin or Paul Monash," he quipped, mentioning the two brightest producers on the television horizon at the time, people he very much admired.

It was soon after that conversation that Quinn Martin offered Burt the chance to star in another police-type television series. This time there would be no Indian image as Burt portrayed Lieutenant Dan August, keeper of the law in a small town. And this time the show would be a joint venture between Quinn Martin and Burt Reynolds' own company, BR Productions.

"Burt has a chance to go right through the roof in this series," was how Quinn Martin put it. "I think he has this image of himself as a dour, strong and silent type and has usually played a little too straight. We'll get some charm and warmth into Dan August, in addition to all that virility. He has all the scope he needs as an actor and his confidence has grown too."

Heading his own company and a new television series was only one of the many ways in which Burt was branching out. He had also gone into the cattle-raising business, putting his father in charge of the more than thirty head of Black Angus that were now roaming the Ranch.

"All they do is eat," he laughed. "That's six thousand dollars a month I spend right there."

While attending a horse auction with his good friend Jim Brolin (of "Marcus Welby" fame), who was breeding and raising Appaloosas, Burt became so intrigued with the idea of owning his own horse-breeding farm that he bid on and bought his first Appaloosa that day.

Back in 1967, a small group of wealthy Palm Beach business-men had shown their pride and admiration in their hometown boy by investing $1,000,000 in a large plot of land, where they planned to construct the Burt Reynolds Playhouse and restaurant. It was to be a part of the pre-Broadway circuit and would seat a thousand people. Soon Burt became involved in helping to raise funds to build the playhouse. Today it draws thousands of people from neighboring towns and whenever Burt appears on stage, the show is an instant sellout.

Despite the failure of his attempts in television and the movies he considered second-rate, Burt's following grew. Audiences saw something in the zealous young man that the supposedly shrewd executives within the industry had missed. Out of gratitude to the school that gave him his start as an actor, Burt established an annual scholarship at his alma mater, Palm Beach Junior College.

His ambition resided of necessity in Hollywood, but his heart has always lived in his hometown state. "I'd rather live in Florida than anywhere," he has often declared.

And to prove that he means just that, Burt heads for his house in Jupiter, Florida and those he loves best whenever he can. That's where this good old country boy is the happiest: with his family, in his *real* home.

Over the years Burt has frequently dated Miko Mayama, a lovely young Japanese actress who had appeared with Charlton Heston in *The Hawaiians*. Lonely and longing to be close to someone with whom he could share his precious moments away from the pressures of the studio, Burt picked up the threads of his friendship with Miko. They often appeared together at parties and other Hollywood social functions and Burt was candid with the press about his "friendship" for Miko. While the fan magazines ran coverline stories speculating as to whether they might get married, Burt merely shrugged. He was definitely not of a marriage mind.

But by the start of the 1970 fall season, when "Dan August" first aired, rumor had it that Miko was living in Burt's home on Miller Drive above Sunset Boulevard, cozily tucked away in the house behind the great wrought-iron gates bearing the huge letter "R" in the center. Despite his tremendous charismatic appeal to women and the Don Juan reputation manufactured by overimaginative writers, Burt has always been a one-woman

39

man. For all his adult life he has preferred a one-to-one relationship, so it was not surprising that he was spending his free time with Miko, a woman he greatly admired. He was comfortable with her, something a constant change of romantic partners makes impossible. Reporters continued to question his plans for a deeper commitment and Burt, always cooperative with the press, assured them that he was not going to marry Miko. He admired her, enjoyed her company. That was all.

They respected his candid reply.

In an effort to win a viewing audience for "Dan August," it was necessary to promote the show before and well into the new fall season. Burt was scheduled to appear on "The Merv Griffin Show" to discuss the series. He had never been *himself* in front of a camera, not even in that early personality test that had been a dismal failure. He was nervous and uncertain about how to act. Then, just before Merv announced Burt as his next guest, he took a deep breath and decided impulsively to wing it.

Suddenly the viewers saw a different Burt Reynolds emerge. He was no longer the grim, unsmiling, steely-eyed, ruggedly handsome man he portrayed on the screen. He was, instead, a man of great wit and warmth. The real Burt was the antithesis of his celluloid image.

"I've become the Dody Goodman of the talk shows," he said. "The audience is shocked because I'm just being me. The important thing on a talk show is to make people like you," he explained to those who expressed surprise at his sudden popularity in a kind of show he had never tried before.

Burt Reynolds was not only a talented actor, he was the kind of person you would want for a friend. Men *and* women adored him. Men wanted to look like him, to exude that macho essence that seemed to ooze from every pore. Women wanted to look *at* him, to delight in the approval that gleamed in his dark eyes. He was every man's secret idol, every woman's fantasy lover. He now had an entirely different, adoring public at his beck and call.

In February, together with Jim Brolin and his wife Jane, Burt and Miko attended the Foreign Press Awards. The Beverly Hilton Hotel was filled with screaming women who were unable to contain themselves as Burt walked up the red carpet waving to the crowd behind the roped-off section. He had been nominated for a Golden Globe, for best actor in the television series "Dan August," a sure sign that he was on his way at last. This time, he hoped, there would be no detours.

A week later the cast and crew of "Dan August" were on hiatus and Burt anxiously awaited word on the fate of the show. Would it be picked up for the new season? Feeling optimistic about his future, Burt bought himself a gift of a bright red, two-seater Mercedes. He and pal Norman Fell, who played his side-kick in the series, drove down to La Costa, a posh hotel/spa thirty miles north of San Diego.

Burt and Miko had spent a weekend there in November and he had thoroughly enjoyed the relaxing surroundings of the luxurious resort. Determined to set aside all concern about the fate of "Dan August," he and Norman planned to work out in the gym and just enjoy the amenities the hotel offered. He had agreed to do a photo layout for a leading magazine, but for the rest of the time Burt planned to indulge in his favorite pastimes: room service and watching television. It was the perfect way to unwind after months of long, hard hours on the set.

However, there was one admirer who would not accept the fact that Burt wanted to spend some time alone. She began phoning him from Los Angeles asking if she should come down. Burt politely declined her offer. Throughout the afternoon the calls continued.

That evening Burt dined with Norman and another friend who was also visiting La Costa for a short time. Twice during dinner Burt was called away to the phone. Each time he returned his annoyance was evident, but he did not mention the name of his caller, just that she was someone he had taken out once. It was typical of him to show consideration for someone who was certainly not doing the same for him.

Fearing that she might make good on her threat and wanting to avoid an unpleasant scene if she did, Burt took refuge in a friend's suite, where they talked and watched television for the rest of the evening.

His effect on women has always been potent. Burt understands and respects women. He has never been heard to make a chauvinistic remark, even in jest. His admiration for women in general dates back to one woman in particular: his mother.

"I do like women. Women have been nice to me from my

mother on down. They have been terrific," he has stated frankly.

"Quite honestly I think that most men don't really *like* women. They'd rather talk and tell jokes and play pool, confess, drink beer, and even cry with a man. I've always found that if you have the right relationship, you can have all those things with a woman.

"It isn't the physical things about a woman that turn me on," he continued. "It's that subtle touch—the way a woman puts her hand on a man's arm or the way she crosses her legs—that tells it all. It's more of a sensual thing than strictly boobs or legs. Talking, if it's done well, turns me on. There are innuendos that can pass between a man and a woman that are obvious only to the two of them, so that even with other people around, only they are aware of what's really happening.

"Being comfortable with a woman and making *her* feel comfortable is the key to a good relationship. The kick I get is what *I can give*. I can't possibly have a relationship with someone just for my own pleasure. I like aggressive women. I like career women.

"What I get out of a relationship is what I give."

CHAPTER EIGHT

urt's first stop upon his return from La Costa on Wednesday afternoon was at a television studio, where he reported for the taping of "The Dinah Shore Show." In those years Dinah devoted most of her on-camera time to chatting with her guests while she prepared their favorite dishes. Being a true southerner, Burt shared her passion for pecan pie and other southern specialties. But it was not Dinah's culinary expertise that sparked Burt's interest on that first meeting. It was soon evident to everyone on the set that something special was happening between them; the vibration of mutual attraction was loud and clear.

Those who saw the show weeks later thought it very amusing when Burt (by prearrangement with the producer) jumped out of a closet as Dinah opened the door. She was clearly surprised, but the smile on her face gave away her approval of the "trick" Burt and her producer had played on her. With his usual spontaneous humor, Burt threatened to kill himself if Dinah didn't go out with him; then he proceeded to take a nosedive onto a breakway table while Dinah stared.

"She didn't say anything for about eight minutes. Just stood there looking at this crazy person," he remembers.

By the time he had left the studio and headed for his home above Sunset Boulevard, he had already begun a new and exciting chapter in his life. For a long time friends and co-workers had been telling him that Dinah was an ardent admirer of his and wanted to meet him. "She thinks you're terrific. She wants you to be on her show," they insisted.

Burt shrugged off their remarks, refusing to take them seriously. Why would Dinah Shore be so anxious to meet him? She had plenty of guys to choose from. But now that they had met officially, Burt had second thoughts on the matter. He was attracted to Dinah, of that there was no doubt. There was an immediate chemistry between them that he could not deny. Dinah was fun. She understood and appreciated his somewhat caustic sense of humor and was able to match his wit with razor-sharp comebacks of her own. They complemented one another.

Yet he was reluctant to begin a new relationship. Old hurts still festered; wounds that hadn't healed still chafed. He was not quite ready for a new love, at least not one that would be as meaningful as he felt it must inevitably be with this very special woman.

A few days later, at the end of February, Burt received word that "Dan August" had been cancelled. After only seventeen episodes his big chance had turned into yet another defeat.

That same night he appeared, all smiles, on "The Merv Griffin Show." He made a point of telling Merv that he had a major announcement to make regarding "Dan August," and then, grinning like a Cheshire cat, he said, "I've just been canceled." He won over the audience by making a joke of what most actors would consider a disaster. "I have the distinction of being the only actor in the history of TV who has been canceled by all three networks," he chortled.

To himself he thought, now what?

He had once confided to a friend that there were two things he really wanted to do. One was to be on "The Carol Burnett Show" so that he could use his innate, zany sense of humor with a woman he admired greatly, a comedienne par excellence. The other was to be a guest on "The Tonight Show." He longed to exchange quips with Johnny.

Neither of these wishes seemed to be even slightly visible on the horizon as he pondered what direction to take now that his series was over.

"The trouble with Burt was that no one knew how to use his personality," Monte Markham has said of his friend. "They tried to make him an actor-actor, never taking into consideration that Burt is one of those easy-going guys who can laugh his way through a scene better than many who play it moment to moment, from the heart. That's just the way it is with him."

Then, on April 2, 1971, one wish came true. He made a guest appearance on "The Tonight Show" taping in New York. That night Burt parlayed his very special personality into a winner with his first appearance on Johnny Carson's late-night show. The fast-shuffled verbal exchange between the two men drew so much laughter from the audience that it drowned out some of Burt's more pungent remarks. The spontaneous hilarity was such a hit that during the commercial break Johnny invited Burt to return on May 31 as guest host during his absence.

So despite the cancellation of "Dan August," the uncertainty of the direction of his career, things were not so dismal after all.

Nineteen seventy-one had even more surprises in store for an unsuspecting Burt.

The remodeling of his new home was nearly completed. Burt was anxious to get things in order and had already decided on the decor. The house would be done in his favorite colors, black and red. A hand-carved, four-poster bed costing $700 was on order. The house was part of an estate once owned by Arthur Lowe, and Burt had great plans for his life behind the iron gates. Home was his sanctuary, the place where he would unwind, eat pizza, and watch television.

While the repairmen made their final touches so the furnishings could be delivered, Burt headed for Jupiter. There he was able to set aside anxieties about his career for a while. He could ride his motorcycle, go for long walks in the woods, fish in his own lake. And, best of all, he could take the phone off the hook and read contentedly from high up in his tree house. For a while anyway, the pressures abated.

When he returned to Hollywood after his guest-host stint on "The Tonight Show," Burt was puzzled and surprised to find a message from director John Boorman, who wanted to see Burt in his office at Warner Brothers.

Burt was even more surprised by what Boorman wanted to discuss.

"He wanted to talk to me about my being in *Deliverance.*"

Burt was familiar with the book by James Dickey and had heard about the plans to turn it into a film. Now he wondered aloud what the director had ever seen in his films that would have made him think that Burt could play the role of Lewis in this heavy drama.

Boorman's reply was simple. "I saw you on 'The Tonight Show' last week."

Burt could only stare at him in amazement. "But this is not a funny movie. What did you see that made you want me?"

What Boorman saw, he assured Burt, was a man who had shown a rare ability during his stint as guest host on the late-night show. "There were six people on the panel and you were maneuvering them all. You were in control of them. That's what I want in this character."

He then asked if Burt could speak with a southern accent. Burt assured Boorman that despite the twelve years he had spent ridding himself of his homegrown southern drawl, he would be able to pick it up again in a short time.

At last the break he had hoped for had materialized. Burt vowed that he would do everything he could to make this opportunity work. It was a choice role, one that would give him the chance to show his real capabilities.

"Then Jon Voight, whom I'd never met before, walked into the room and we began to improvise and talk. We hit it off," Burt remembers.

Within a short time he left for the remote location spot in the mountains of northern Georgia where *Deliverance* was to be

45

filmed. He had arranged to fly into New York to do "The To-night Show" on weekends whenever necessary.

A crew of seventy-five actors, technicians, and production people arrived in the backwoods town of Clayton, Georgia, population 985, within days of each other for the summer-long filming of this tense, action-packed drama. Many booked rooms in the only hotel in town; others moved into rented houses, and still others were accommodated at the Kingwood Country Club, a posh golfers' retreat.

Burt and Jon Voight rented cottages on the edge of the pond on the grounds of Kingwood. In no time at all word of their arrival began to draw enthusiastic fans to the location site. They came in boats, on foot, on bicycles, and even in golf carts to catch a glimpse of *real* movie stars. Women of all ages parked in Burt's driveway. They hung around unashamedly outside his trailer dressing room, even attempting at times to crash closed sets. Burt, while open and friendly, pretended not to notice the extent to which some of his more extroverted fans went to gain his attention. However, there were times when he could not ignore them. "Women would call at three or four in the morning and say 'I'm the girl you're looking for,' " he remembers.

In the meantime, Burt and Dinah had been keeping in touch since his surprise appearance on her show. While they had not yet had an official date, it was obvious to them that it was inevitable. Meanwhile, both were deeply involved in career matters, and romance had to take a back seat.

"She wanted to visit me on location but I said no. I was worried about her image. I didn't know how terribly capable she is of handling anything," he recalls.

Miko, however, made several trips to visit the man she loved, unaware of what was happening between Burt and Dinah, or perhaps unwilling to acknowledge the fact that another woman had come into the picture. She had known and loved Burt for a long time, had hoped that one day he might decided to settle down with her, although he had never given her any real reason to think that he would.

But other things were generating for Burt. Opportunities were tumbling into his lap. The Johnny Carson show had given him a new dimension. He had mastered the putdown, convincing television audiences that he was an outrageously funny man, one they welcomed into their homes. Rumors of his brilliant performance in *Deliverance* filtered down from the banks of the river, where they were filming.

One night on "The Tonight Show," he found himself sitting next to Helen Gurley Brown, editor of *Cosmopolitan*. Mrs. Brown had been conducting a search for a celebrity to be the first male centerfold in an upcoming issue of her magazine.

"As you know," she later commented, "*Cosmopolitan* had been looking for the Perfect Man. Suddenly there he was."

What Mrs. Brown considered perfect was a man who was on the macho side, very good-looking, and heterosexual. The centerfold was planned with much care and secrecy about the man who was to pose for it. Mrs. Brown's campaign to launch the April 1972 issue, which would feature the first all-nude male centerfold, was carried out to perfection. When the issue hit the stands, it was gobbled up by eager, mostly female, readers whose curiosity had been aroused by the pre-publication publicity.

Rumors circulated that some of Hollywood's top male sex symbols, such as Steve McQueen, Clint Eastwood, and football's Joe Namath, had turned down the chance to be *Cosmo*'s centerfold. What transpired between Burt, Mrs. Brown, and David Gershonson (Burt's press agent) we don't really know. But the fact is that both Burt and his press agent thought it would be a good idea, certainly high camp, for Burt to accept Mrs. Brown's offer. What occurred in the months following the publication of *Cosmopolitan*'s April 1972 issue was almost unbelievable.

It has been said that this was the principal turning point in Burt's career. That the centerfold pushed him over the line into superstardom has been an issue of controversy among many, both inside and outside the entertainment industry. Burt has often disagreed with the theory, many times to the point of obvious resentment. Perhaps it was the centerfold that catapulted him before the public eye in a unique and somewhat overt manner. It certainly did not detract from whatever popularity he'd had before the centerfold. But, according to the man who posed for it, the sudden fame that seemed to overwhelm him right after the publication of that issue of *Cosmo* was not solely due to his having the distinction of being the first male centerfold.

The matter is still in debate, much like the chicken and the egg.

CHAPTER NINE

y the end of August 1971, when he returned from the filming site of *Deliverance,* Burt had been on the Carson show a number of times and had also seen the fulfillment of his second wish, to appear on "The Carol Burnett Show." Burt had gleefully romped through hilarious skits with the inimitable Miss Burnett and her talented cast of ribticklers. When Burt lightly tripped down a flight of stairs as he was singing (in a remarkably good voice), it brought down the house. He was gorgeous, he was glib, and he was ridiculously funny. That night Burt gained an entirely new group of admirers who became worshipful fans on the spot.

His second appearance on Dinah Shore's show was at her invitation. On September 14, 1971, the two had their first official date. Rumors of this new romance had already infiltrated the gossip columns, but neither of the two parties had discussed their relationship for publication. Each seemed to be treading very carefully.

Dinah had been deeply hurt by the breakup of her seventeen-year marriage to George Montgomery. Although she was a frequent partygoer and was often photographed with various eligible men, she had been carefully guarding her heart for a long time.

Slowly the truth was revealed as their dates could no longer be kept hidden from the constantly alert, ever-present press. This May–December love affair was fodder for them. Much was made of the sixteen-year age difference by everyone but Burt, who stated quite frankly that he didn't know Dinah's true age, nor did he care. That the two were a beautiful couple was never disputed.

"At first I thought that it took Dinah an incredible amount of courage to admit what was going on between us, but I understand how it's really a part of everything she is," Burt commented during an interview. "Carol Burnett and Dinah are the two women in the industry I've never heard anyone bad-mouth. A week went by, then six months, and we were still together."

However, there was someone else still lingering in Burt's life. Someone he didn't want to hurt.

Miko's career was at a standstill. She was a talented actress but had not done much to further her career, preferring instead to bask in the success of the man to whom she was devoted. They had shared many beautiful moments and she knew that Burt truly cared for her. She had stood by in the past, waiting patiently, when he gave his affections to someone else, and she was certain that once again he would return to her when this romantic interlude was over.

She could not foresee the strength and endurance of Burt and Dinah's love for one another.

She was not alone in her assumption that this too would pass in a short time. Many of Burt's friends wondered how the romance would stand up under the pressure of a demanding press who seemed to devour every bit of information about them and were constantly on the alert for a public appearance of the country's newest and most intriguing duo. Ex-wife Judy Carne was among the few who wondered aloud, making her own observation about the new twosome. She was reported to have phoned Burt to tell him her opinion of his romance with Dinah.

"I know she's a lovely lady," she told a columnist. "But let's talk about age. Dinah's fifty-one. Burt's in his early thirties." (He was in fact thirty-five.)

Judy was recuperating from the breakup of her second marriage as well as the tumble her own career had taken, and there was speculation as to the motivation behind her phone call to Burt.

"Burt's matured as I have. If two people as strong as we could ever get it all together between them, they could have the world."

An acquaintance recalls how once, early in 1971, seeing Judy on a television commercial, Burt had wailed, "Darling, what are you doing?"

But he paid no heed to her frank dismay over his relationship with Dinah.

He was the object of innumerable requests for interviews. The subject of Dinah was always brought up. At first he was reluctant to discuss what he considered a very private matter. But after a while he realized that it was not something either he or Dinah could keep in swaddling cotton for very long.

"I was terribly lucky to have met her at the crossroads of her life. I'm sure she wouldn't have been the same if I had met her ten years ago. She knows exactly what she wants. She refuses to spend any time on anything that's going to hurt or bore."

He was perturbed and understandably hurt by those who insisted, however subtly, that the relationship was to his benefit alone. "I made a half million dollars last year," he said at one point, "so I don't need her for my career. And she certainly doesn't need me for hers. But nobody points that out."

How true. The focal point of any story on Burt and Dinah was always the glaring age gap between them. That Dinah looked radiantly youthful no matter what her age, that she was a superb figure of a woman, that Burt was many years wiser and emotionally more mature than the average thirty-five-year-old—these points were never mentioned. The truth was that neither of them ever gave a thought to the age difference. What they did think about were the similarities between them, those comfortable areas where they were enough alike to make their relationship work in perfect harmony.

"I know what he expects of me as a woman. And my being southern means a lot to Burt's father," Dinah remarked.

According to Dinah these similarities included the fact that both were bundles of energy who could continue all day on a whirlwind of hectic pace and then suddenly be eager for a quiet evening at home.

"It's a big chore for us to go out," said Dinah. "You wouldn't believe how nervous we are at something like a premiere. We smile a lot, but . . ."

While Burt tended to skim over their relationship when confronted by questioning reporters, Dinah was open and frank. "Burt looks like he knows it all, but behind that is a vulnerable, sensitive man."

Somewhat ill at ease about discussing it, Burt reluctantly admitted that he and Dinah had made a pact in the beginning. "We would just make the best of it for as long as it lasted. Be honest with each other for as long as it lasted. If that was forever—terrific. If not, we didn't want to hurt each other.

"It's a relationship that isn't totally what it seems to be. I think it could go on forever no matter what happens. And that's something I've never had before. If everything stopped tomorrow between us, I would never want to lose Dinah as a friend. And I don't think I ever could. Every other time I've ever been in love or had a relationship with a woman, it has ended like a bomb and then it would take time to get it all together again. But it wouldn't be that way with Dinah," he prophesied.

Within a few weeks after the completion of *Deliverance,* Burt began a dizzy whirlwind of moviemaking. His schedule was so busy he barely had time to enjoy his "new" home in the Hollywood Hills. First he did *Fuzz* with Raquel Welch, with whom it was rumored he did not work in complete harmony, and directly afterward he went into the filming of *Shamus* on location in Brooklyn. Between films he managed to appear in the play *Nobody Loves an Albatross* in a theater just outside Chicago.

In the spring of 1972, just as the famous, eagerly awaited centerfold was being grabbed off the newsstands throughout the country, Burt was on location. A horde of screaming women descended upon him in Brooklyn, where he was preparing to do a street scene for *Shamus.* It was at that point that Burt effected a clever way of handling what was to become a recurrent happening—impassioned women demanding his attention, sometimes rudely but always fervently. It could easily have become a touchy situation if not for Burt's quick-witted approach.

"If you turn and run away down the street they're going to run right after you," he remarked. "If you stand there and just give them your best virile look and your phone number they'll think you're an ass." Instead, Burt, aware of the necessity to respect the dignity of his ardent fans, took the time to laugh with them and gently kid them about their reverence for his movie-star image. Thus he endeared himself to thousands of women who might otherwise have felt put down and hurt for being ignored or patronized.

It was the first issue of *Cosmopolitan* ever to sell out completely. Ninety-eight percent of that month's issues had already been sold within two days after it appeared on the stands. According to a memo from the Circulation head of the Hearst Corporation (publishers of *Cosmopolitan*), some newsstand owners reported that customers had used razor blades to slice the insert of Burt from the magazine.

A two-headed monster was now dominating his life. No one, not even Burt, could deny that the centerfold had generated nationwide publicity, which brought him instant recognition that set him well apart from other actors. Film offers began to pour into his office, scripts that were sent to him first rather than after some other "big name" had turned them down. But there were repercussions that later made Burt wonder if he had really used good judgment in agreeing to pose for what had become an internationally famous photo.

In her March 23 column in *The Los Angeles Times,* Hollywood reporter Joyce Haber stated that Burt was dodging the press at his temporary headquarters in Arlington, Illinois, where he was appearing with Lois Nettleton in *The Rainmaker.*

That had been the first inkling of the furor that would be unleashed when the centerfold was finally unveiled, so to speak.

"Time, Newsweek, the Associated Press have all tried to get me but I haven't talked to anybody," Burt was quoted as having told Miss Haber when he took her call.

Realizing the impact the centerfold would have on the women of America, the press badgered both Reynolds and his press agent for a statement. Instead he remained incommunicado except for his stage appearances.

Helen Gurley Brown was not reticent about the subject, however, and spoke freely about the man in the centerfold. "He's a rising star," she said. "He's got a beautiful body and he's adorable."

His parents, usually in the background, were very proud of Burt's popularity. During the hysteria of the centerfold, Mrs. Reynolds had said, "He does have so many things to do, but

52

he's never too busy to keep in touch. And I'm proud of him. I'm proud of the centerfold. I'm just sorry that I don't have a copy of the picture. We had two copies at home but somehow they've just disappeared."

She basked comfortably in the glow of her son's career. It was nice to know that Buddy was doing so well at what he wanted to do and still had his feet on the ground.

"He's a good boy," she said lovingly.

Burt finally made a statement. He had agreed to pose free of charge for his own reasons. "I did it because it was fun and funky and a good sendup for *Playboy* and all its male chauvinist nonsense. I don't take this sex-symbol stuff seriously. I rather doubt that chicks in the roller derby are going to paste me up on their lockers. I expect a lot of girls to be turned off by it."

Burt had given final approval of the photo to be used, and he was very unhappy when a different shot of him folded out from the magazine in late March. Although the afternoon photo session in the fall of 1971 had been something of a lark, with Burt being plied with vodka-laced drinks to unleash any latent inhibitions he might have, the result was not.

By then his romance with Dinah was firmly established. The two were so much an item that one could not say one of their names without quickly adding the other. In an early interview Dinah gave her feelings on their relationship with candor. "We both like to observe other people and what makes their buttons go. We're both family oriented. We both hate arguments of any kind."

In the midst of his hectic filmmaking, the surge of popularity, and stage appearances, he found time to recharge at his ranch in Jupiter, where Dinah would putter about in the tree house kitchen, cooking hushpuppies and frying fish for her man.

"Just walking on land that is mine, seeing my parents happy, watching my nieces and nephews running around. Catching up with old friends, swimming in the creek. All those corny things make me happy," Burt remarked.

That and having a woman like Dinah in his life.

Friends and co-workers had reservations about his over-zealous pursuit of his career. A man could drive himself only so hard, they whispered among themselves. Some went as far as to cautiously warn Burt of the consequences to his health. But the warnings went unheeded until Burt could no longer ignore them.

"I'm a workaholic," he admitted. "Making movies is my outlet." Despite his rise to superstardom, Burt had not yet learned to turn down a script.

One longtime associate remarked that Burt had been in his home so little that he had barely had time to get his bathing trunks wet in the Olympic-sized pool.

The house was not empty, however. Miko was still living there.

As the relationship between Burt and Dinah deepened, Miko refused to believe that Burt would not return to her. She had waited for him before and continued to do so now despite the growing awkwardness of the situation. On his infrequent visits to Los Angeles, Burt would spend most of his time in Dinah's Bel Air mansion. And, as he moved from location to location on the movie marathon he had scheduled, Dinah's visits to the location sites were well chronicled by the press. She would arrive all smiles, her upbeat personality generating sunshine over everyone. Her appearances were balm to an often weary Burt.

Dinah and Miko had never met. Neither spoke of the other in Burt's presence. He was aware that each knew of the other and, caught between the two women, he could not help feeling somewhat bewildered. How could he unravel this tangle, he wondered? Burt is a soft-hearted man who has never been able to willfully bring hurt to another person. Yet he was in love with Dinah and although she had said little or nothing about it, he knew that Dinah was not comfortable with the fact that another woman was living in his home, even though he wasn't there.

In the spring of 1972, after wrapping up a "Hollywood Squares" taping, Burt took off for his ranch in Jupiter. When he returned to his home in Los Angeles a couple of weeks later, all evidence of Miko's having ever lived there was gone. Still he did not just forget her or the fact that they had spent many wonderful times together. He was not a man to forget any person who had been a friend, and Miko had been that.

Not long afterwards the announcement of Miko's engagement reached Burt. Her future husband was said to be a prominent businessman. Burt was happy for her, pleased that she would be starting a new life with someone who loved her.

He was soon caught up in the backlash of the centerfold. His reaction to the photo that had been used instead of the one he had approved was frank disappointment.

"I look like I've been studying humility with Gene Barry. I prefer the shot where I was laughing at myself. Now I'm just smugly smiling."

Some said that it was just the strain of feeling self-conscious now that the photo had been published. Reality had taken over in place of the joke Burt had thought it would be when he'd agreed to be the *Cosmo* playboy.

Dinah had seen the photos prior to publication. "She saw the humor in it," Burt explained. "I'll tell you, if she had thought it was awful, I'd have thought twice about going through with this."

The lady he always referred to as "very classy" proved just how classy she was when she told a reporter in no uncertain terms, "I don't think it does him justice."

There he lay, sprawled across the bearskin rug, looking very comfortable—his head propped up on one hand, the other arm draped discreetly across his body, a cigar in his mouth, a grin on his face.

Shortly after the initial hubbub of the centerfold publication, Burt was playing a love scene with Lois Nettleton in *The Rainmaker* when something significant occurred. As Burt began to remove the hairpins from his co-star's hair in preparation for the scene to follow, the audience in the Arlington, Illinois, playhouse grew hushed. They sighed in unison as the scene progressed. One woman is said to have become so overwhelmed that she rushed out of the suburban theater. Another rose to her feet and began to shout, "Take it off, take it off."

After the performance, as Burt was cheerfully signing autographs and joking with the women who gushed around him, an eighty-year-old woman handed him a long-stemmed rose. Looking her straight in the eye, in a tone of great seriousness, Burt inquired, "Tell me, do you fool around?" He adored them all. They were his public. And who was he to sneer at that kind of admiration?

But not everyone was kind and adoring. There were those who, out of jealousy, pique, or whatever, insisted that he had had other reasons to do the centerfold than "just for a lark." There were those who labeled him "strange," an exhibitionist, or who said that he had been paid a great deal of money.

In one instance, someone in a beauty salon was heard to remark that in reality Burt was actually not well-endowed, the reason for his hand covering a strategic area. A young woman overhearing the remark promptly walked over to the tittering person who had made the statement and in no uncertain terms told him what to do with his unsubstantiated gossip.

"I know from personal experience," she glowered, "that you are full of shit."

The woman's name has never been revealed, only that she had dated Burt intimately a couple of times.

With his usual aplomb, Burt managed to turn what could have been a nightmare into a positive experience. As the innuendo and jokes continued he began to join in with his own putdowns.

"I kept turning down lots of money to do other things, calendars, et cetera. I knew that I couldn't take money and still maintain that I'd done the centerfold for a joke. Who would have believed me?"

He kidded about it on the Carson show and made quips to the press. He even agreed to autograph and personally deliver a copy of the centerfold to the highest bidder at a "Fight for Sight" charity auction benefit. Eventually even those who had raised their eyebrows in question about this "strange-behaving actor" had been won over. They had begun to see Burt for what he was, a sincere and very funny guy.

What pleased him most, however, was the fact that he was finally getting scripts that were not rejects from better-known actors. His sense of humor was in full force and going strong when he agreed to appear in a segment of Woody Allen's *Everything You Always Wanted to Know About Sex . . .* in the role of a sperm. By early August he was on location again, this time in Little Rock, Arkansas, for the filming of *White Lightning* under the direction of Joe Sargent, who said of him, "He has the same kind of craft as McQueen and Newman."

Despite the craziness following the publication of *Cosmo*'s centerfold, Burt agreed to pose again, bare-chested, for an upcoming issue of *Esquire.* He was not going to take himself seriously.

What disturbed him most was that people were saying his new career status was due largely to the surge of popularity brought about by the centerfold. "I was receiving five thousand letters a week before then," he protested. *"Deliverance* was shot and ready for release before the photo came out in *Cosmopolitan.* It's just that it all came to a head at the same time. If people want to say that the bearskin bit was the reason for all this, let them say it. It's like saying you scored the touchdown because all the other guys were on their knees. I don't care. I scored and won. You have to do things that are first. *I don't want to be second.* I've had that all my life."

Yet despite that strong statement, it did rankle that some people did not give him credit for anything other than a lot of muscles and brawn. But in the long run he has had the last laugh on all of the doubters and the scoffers.

CHAPTER TEN

"I think he's the kind of man I'd dig spending a long night with, followed by an even longer matinee," said one dishy admirer of the *Cosmo* Playboy of the Month, Burt Reynolds.

In Chicago, while appearing in *The Rainmaker,* the man of the hour again displayed his genuine respect for the bevy of adoring women who sighed after him. In a gesture of great generosity, Burt treated a large group of female fans to a little after-theater party complete with a kiss for each of them, hors d'oeuvres, and champagne. No doubt all seventy women are still in a glow remembering that event.

"A man gave me a check for eight hundred dollars to kiss his wife and have drinks with her in a Texas restaurant. I kissed her three times, got smashed, and gave the money to charity," Burt told a reporter during an interview in the wake of the centerfold.

But what began as a lark, a sardonic putdown of *Playboy* magazine, was soon backfiring. Life had become a fishbowl. His every move was watched by eager fans. "Everything started to converge on me at once. I couldn't leave my hotel room. I thought to myself, 'Maybe I don't want it [fame] that bad.' "

As success continued to draw him closer within its exclusive circle, Burt worried about the possible consequences.

"I worry, will I be able to keep the people I care about close to me. I hope I can really enjoy the fame, take it and run with it. It'd kill me to be an unhappy success."

That didn't seem likely. Burt's deep-rooted sense of caring, his genuine concern for those he loved, and his habit of touching base with the basics whenever he could, kept his feet on the ground despite adulation that would have turned the head of many another man. It takes a certain amount of self-awareness to keep a successful person from taking off on an ego trip. And Burt seems to have maintained just that self-awareness.

During the filming of *White Lightning*, Hal Needham's marriage fell apart. Hal had moved into the home of another stuntman who was also separated from his wife. One day while on location in Little Rock, Arkansas, Hal learned that he would have to move out of his new quarters because his friend was reconciling with his wife.

"I was telling Burt that as soon as we got back to town I'd have to find myself an igloo," Hal recalls, "and Burt said, 'Hell, I've got that big house. Why not come over and spend a week or two? It'll give you time to find a place.' "

Hal moved into the guest quarters of Burt's home on the former Arthur Lowe estate above Sunset Boulevard, the house with the bright red carpet ("red makes me feel good"), where the two batched together compatibly. Burt never mentioned anything to Hal about finding another place to live, so, in fact, Hal Needham became a part of the Reynolds household for many years.

On September 14, 1972, Burt and Dinah quietly celebrated their first anniversary together with dinner at a Hollywood restaurant. The relationship with Dinah had become the topic of much speculation. Burt bristled under some of it.

"I know what people think: What's a virile-looking stud like me doing with an older woman like Dinah, a Hollywood legend. Well, the fact is I consider myself terribly lucky to be as close as I am to Dinah. I can tell you there isn't a man in California with any brains who wouldn't give his right arm to be where I am. I've received from Dinah as much as I've given. We're good for each other.

"Dinah is chicken soup. She's exciting and she's funny. She's got great, great taste. Until Dinah, I never had a custom-made suit. She is nice and caring. Everybody talks about her talent and incredible career, but they ignore how really bright, really smart she is," Burt enthused about the woman he loved.

"Dinah was surrounded by a group that was intellectually beyond anything I had ever been a part of. And as clever and cute as I thought I was, I wasn't sure I could be interesting through a whole dinner party," he admitted.

The constant emphasis on the age difference between them chafed. "The press made me out to be a gigolo at the age of thirty-eight. But I did hold my own with those people and I got more confidence, more aware of who I was and what I was and what I could do. For that I thank Dinah."

On December 9, 1972, Burt attended (alone) the Golden Apple Awards luncheon given by the Hollywood Women's Press Club. He had been nominated, along with three other actors, as Star of the Year. Although he didn't win, he was honored by the nomination from a group of women to whom he meant more than just a nude form on a bear rug.

"I think most women understood it [the centerfold] but it misfired also with some," he said.

By the latter part of 1972, he had had more than second thoughts about the aftermath of his photo session.

Deliverance had been released in October, and the admiration and praise from critics and other skeptics inside and outside the industry were music to Burt's ears. Earlier in the year, word had filtered down that Burt's performance in the film would surprise a great many people. It did just that.

His performance in *Deliverance* showed yet another dimension of his talent; he was proving himself to be a man of many facets.

Once again Burt had proven there was much more to the man than the macho facade. He was jubilant. But the continuous questions, the never-ending emphasis on the bearskin-rug episode, cast a shadow over his film triumph. People still didn't fully accept him as an actor. They recognized his talent, but it was more pleasing to recognize him as a cutup, a man who poked fun at everything, especially himself.

He threatened to sue *Cosmopolitan* in mid-November, when he learned that some two million centerfold posters had been sold without his okay. He was furious and minced no words in admitting his anger.

"I used to get bored reading about people suing and I'd say, 'Why did the silly S.O.B. do it in the first place,' but this is getting so far out of hand I've finally had it."

Burt had stood all he could of the centerfold business, and wanted nothing more than to forget it had ever happened. Enough was enough!

Somewhere along the way, Burt made the sentimental gesture of buying the house he had lived in as a boy. "I'm a romantic," he has admitted on a number of occasions.

That romanticism, the core of sentimentality that lies deep within him, is what shines through the surface cockiness. It is what women sense about him—he feels things with every fiber of his being and is not ashamed to admit to those powerful surges of deep emotion.

"If I tell a woman I get high on sunsets, it's corny, but she knows what I mean. It's that I'm trying to share what's inside. It's easy for a guy to be physical—to do the sports bit. But you can't fake feeling. Women simply aren't impressed with masculinity. Men don't listen to women. They say 'I don't trust women.' How are women supposed to prove themselves trustworthy? They're fed a lot of meaningless information about a man's world that is supposed to impress them.

"The real problem between men and women is that everyone is trying so desperately to find out what your act is. Like the Hollywood actor bit: 'Are you *ménage à trois* or *whips?*' There's no attempt to discover what's in a person's head. Men usually treat a woman as a sex object or as another man," he expounded in a 1972 interview, shortly after the centerfold. "I'm not good with women who are swingers. I don't like what they do. I don't like what they represent. And I find them disgustingly boring. My idea of a good time with a woman is to hole up for three days and watch old movies, eat pizza, be silly, act like children, get the giggles. In lots of ways I'm square," he said.

"I'm lucky to have met up with givers. Unfortunately, we're pretty well divided up into givers and takers. The men usually are the takers, the women are the givers. And if all the men whom women meet are takers, the women turn into pathetic givers or into even worse takers themselves," he philosophized. "But it's also a matter of knowing when to give. Lots of times, I'm too tired or too angry or too hurt to be able to give, and that's when I need a woman who knows when to give."

Dinah seemed to have that rare instinct of knowing when Burt was feeling down. He had always insisted that he preferred older women. "Women don't really get their heads together until they're thirty-five," he said. "When I get down in the dumps I like to be alone. I don't like to share with anyone. Just work it out."

A younger woman might feel offended, hurt, left out. But Dinah understood Burt's moods, and she was comfortable to be with.

"I'm not a superstud, though I'm labeled as one. The reason I get myself into these kinds of situations is because I talk too much," he said, referring to his frequent offbeat remarks on talk shows. "But I like being a romantic. Because I am one, I never flirt. When I'm with someone, even if I liked another woman in the room, I would never do anything about it. I never have and I never will. Flirting has the context of being false. There's nothing behind it. I find that in order for anything to work with me it has to come out of a sense of fun and truth. That's why when I'm with someone, no matter how long or short the time is, I am definitely with *her.* There has to be sincerity in everything I do. I can't do it otherwise. I have no ability to fake it. When I'm bored I look it. When I'm uptight, I show it. I can't even put on a happy loser's face at an awards show when I lose.

"I know I'm a paradox. It's because most people aren't as

lucky as I am. I live a very full and happy life. I'm grateful for that but the other side of me tends to become square and humdrum at times."

That side of him, the side he refers to as square and humdrum, liked nothing better than to hide away at his ranch for a few days of down-home fun. By the close of 1972, his single purchase of an Appaloosa had grown into ownership of a number of Arabian and Appaloosa show horses. There were goats roaming the pasture, and Burt had built a tennis court on the ranch for his special lady.

"I've been forced to play tennis," he explained. "I'm going with a jock." He was very proud of Dinah's natural athletic ability and her good sportsmanship.

An enthusiastic painter, Dinah had gotten Burt interested enough to try painting himself. The two often spent long hours at their easels while on the ranch.

"We sit on the porch [of the tree house] and paint. Sometimes we go to the beach. When we do see people at the ranch it's usually my brother and his family or my folks or a couple of my friends.

"I suppose it's a new kind of life for her. I would hope so. But the most important thing is that Dinah makes me feel like it's new and exciting to her. Most of the time we really don't do that much. We just kinda pick each other's brains. I don't think Dinah misses the big parties. I like the fact that she'll ride with me. I'm sure that secretly she has always wanted to ride a motorcycle.

"She is really gutsy," he said. "We were down at the ranch and she took some fall, really bad. The whole side of her face was bleeding. She got up and I said, 'You wanna get back on or you wanna cry?' and she got back on. The next day we went out and she fell again and then again. She was doing what I was doing because she's gutsy as hell and I was letting her because she's a damn good athlete. But she got too confident too fast and so did I. I figured she's great. We're ready to go off in the woods on the bikes. Then she didn't make a corner and almost went off into the canal. The second time she went over the handlebars. The third time she said, 'I quit.'

"I like the idea that she's adopted my family and friends and they've adopted her. I like the fact that she can go out with three stuntmen and me and have a good time. I like the fact that she'll give up a tennis tournament in Beverly Hills or New York to visit me on location. I like the fact that she's a woman who is still a romanticist despite what she's had thrown at her in life. I have enormous respect for her, probably more than I've ever had for any woman in my life."

She was his love, his friend, the woman most important to him during this period of his life.

In an interview given by Dinah to a well-known Hollywood journalist, she is quoted as saying:

"An interesting man is interested in something besides himself. Some men are not. A sensuous man is a man who doesn't turn on to every women he comes in contact with. A complete rover has to be an insecure man. A sensuous man to me has to be kind of secure basically. Burt is the kind of man you could study for ages, and just when you think you know him, he'll turn around and do something that will completely confuse you. Burt is the most unpredictable man I have ever met and that's one of the reasons he's one of the world's most attractive men."

She was tuned in, quick to sense his needs and to answer them when necessary. Dinah seemed to have a kind of built-in sensitivity that told her exactly when to do what. It is part of her natural charm.

"You have to keep your interests alive as far as your man goes, and keep them surging," she advised women in a magazine feature.

"You keep yourself looking young with exercise, take care with what you eat, what you think, and what you feel. You have to make a man feel he is the most important thing in your life. Act as though he is your first love and there's no other man in the world except him. Too many women today take their men for granted."

They were two sides to a whole and together they were a perfect match.

After a brief rest period at the ranch following *White Lightning,* the two returned home, where Burt taped a Flip Wilson show and made an appearance on Dinah's TV special.

His next film, *The Man Who Loved Cat Dancing,* was due to start shooting on location in Gila Bend, Arizona, shortly after the first of January, 1973. It was to mark the beginning of a period of strife and havoc from which he was to suffer for a long time afterwards. In those following months Burt was tested far beyond his darkest dreams. And the woman he loved was to share with him many hours of anguish and despair.

It was a time when friendships, love, and personal courage were tested, and somehow endured.

CHAPTER ELEVEN

In an interview with syndicated columnist Marilyn Beck in July 1972, Dinah had spoken candidly of her relationship with Burt. Ms. Beck observed in her column that Dinah had never looked lovelier.

"I'm having more fun out of life now than I did ten years ago," said the exuberant hostess of NBC's "Dinah's Place," a hit daytime show since it first aired in 1970.

Life hadn't always been kind to this now joyous woman, but it was not Dinah's habit to dwell on the negatives. She had gone from a supposedly good marriage of nearly eighteen years to a short-lived, disastrous marriage to building contractor Maurice Smith, from whom she was divorced in 1966.

"I had been married all my life, it seemed. And suddenly I was alone. And in limbo. I isolated myself from the world, made the mistake of alienating myself from longtime friends. I buried myself in activities with my children [a daughter and adopted son], played tennis and golf, then more tennis and golf. It was a terrible scene. I was so bad. Really. I don't care what anyone thinks—immediate family isn't enough. There's a great big beautiful world out there. And you've got to force yourself to take part in it."

She did not date during those three years of readjustment. Her reason was simple and certainly understandable for any woman who has experienced bitter disappointment in personal relationships. "I was afraid to fall in love again. You reach a point where you're all bottled up, won't allow yourself to give to anyone else. And that's a dangerous thing. Because a big part of living is giving.

"Love?" she queried. "You wait until it finds you. You force the issue, you become nervous because time is passing you by, and good things never happen. You simply have to believe, really believe, that the years aren't important, that you should let things roll as they will. And everything will fall into place."

And fall into place it did when Burt and Dinah realized how important their relationship was. Around her neck she wore a gold medallion inscribed, TO BIG D, LOVE BURT.

Dinah stood her ground and by her actions proved that her words had been more than mere platitudes.

Burt's career continued to move at a fast pace and some worried that it was too fast. However, Burt had always been in great physical condition. Except for the automobile accident in 1955 and the knee surgery in 1969, he had managed to steer clear of any major health problems. Many attributed his optimum health during that period of his life to the good influence of the woman in his life. Dinah was an image of fitness herself, and there were those who thought she had made Burt more conscious of proper nutrition. Whatever the reason, he was looking better than ever and feeling as great as he looked.

More open about the relationship with Dinah now that it had gone into its third year, Burt said of her, "I'm not seeing other ladies because she's all I can handle."

During the *six*-day run of *The Rainmaker* in a Toledo, Ohio, playhouse he earned the same amount of money he had been paid for *seven weeks* of production on "Dan August," when he had put in twelve to fourteen hours per working day.

His investments had stretched to include a couple of parcels of land, which were in the process of being developed into a self-contained community near Little Rock, Arkansas, where he had filmed two features. He had caught the brass ring, but by the second week in February 1973, that brass ring had begun to show evidence of tarnish, as events beyond Burt's control converged upon him in a nightmare that was to create a living hell.

MGM was filming the best-selling novel, *The Man Who Loved Cat Dancing*, written by Marilyn Durham. The production notes issued by the studio described the film as "a blend of love story and high adventure set in the American West of the 1880's." Producer Martin Poll had purchased the movie rights from the first-time author and, with a screenplay adaptation by top film writer Eleanor Perry, had signed Burt Reynolds to play the role of ex-cavalry officer Jay Grobart, and English actress Sarah Miles (*Ryan's Daughter*) to play his romantic interest, Catherine Crocker. Others in the stellar cast included Lee J. Cobb, Jack Warden, and George Hamilton. Filming began on location in the rugged terrain of Arizona.

It was Burt's sixth film since the demise of "Dan August," his first screen love story. For Sarah Miles it was also a first—a made-in-America film. And it was Martin Poll's first Western. Little did anyone imagine that it would be a first in a more dramatic way for everyone connected with the film. And, for some, its aftershock would be felt for a very long time.

At the end of January the cast and crew of the film were hard at work in the remote location site of Gila Bend, Arizona. During the many weeks of filming, the company experienced a variety of weather difficulties: dust storms, flash floods, heavy rains, and even hail. In addition, both Reynolds and Miles, as well as Jack Warden, were insistent upon doing their own stunts, which placed considerable demands upon them. Burt had always done his own stunts even while his stunt double sat nearby. But in the face of the unusual stress due to the weather and the physical action called for in the screenplay, the filming of *Cat Dancing* was no piece of cake.

When talk-show host Merv Griffin arrived on the set it was almost a relief, for it gave the cast an excuse to party. On the night of the tenth of February they celebrated Griffin's visit and Burt's birthday (on the eleventh) with a dinner party at the Palomino Bar and Restaurant in the nearby town of Ajo. Sarah's business manager and companion at the location shooting, David Whiting, did not attend the party.

According to the news accounts that appeared the following day, the events of the night went something like this:

Sarah Miles became restless and bored with the party, where, as she described it, "all they were doing was eating food." When actor Cobb offered her a ride back to the motel where the cast was quartered during the filming, she accepted. One report states that she and Cobb had a drink and that the actress and he parted company around midnight.

Miles then went to visit Burt, to apologize for leaving his birthday party early. According to later testimony, she found Burt in the midst of a massage. A magazine article quotes Burt as saying, "Yes, Sarah was in my room while I was getting a massage. Massage didn't used to be a dirty word. No, I didn't want Sarah there. I asked her to leave but she wouldn't."

Instead, Sarah is reported to have watched TV, taken a cat nap, and returned to her room around 3 A.M. What occurred then was also recorded by the court.

As Sarah Miles later testified, her business manager, David Whiting, was waiting for her in her room and when she entered immediately began to cross-examine her about where she had been and with whom. Miles described him as threatening and physical as he "began throwing me around the room and shouting, *'If you don't tell me, I'll kill you.'* " When her son's governess heard the scuffle from her adjoining room, she ran in, and Sarah told her to call Burt. By the time he got there from his room at the other end of the motel, Whiting had fled.

Seeing Sarah, who was shaken from the slapping she said Whiting had inflicted upon her, he remarked, "Christ Almighty you're a mess."

He then returned to his room with the actress, who sought sanctuary from her attacker, she later told police.

The following morning when she returned to her room, Miles found David Whiting lying dead on the floor of her bathroom. What followed was like the script of a 1930s mystery, as speculation about the cause of death began to circulate through Gila Bend. As news of the tragedy swept through the nearby towns and into Phoenix, where it was picked up by the wire services, the momentum of the incident was heightened. Soon everyone was guessing at what had happened. Whiting had been known to threaten and even to attempt suicide on previous occasions, so when the county medical examiner testified at an inquest that the twenty-six-year-old man had died of an overdose of drugs, it was no surprise to those who had known him well.

Not content to leave the matter at that, some members of the press and the public were quick to jump on rumors that Whiting's death might not have been due solely to drug overdose. There were ugly innuendoes about the wound found on the back of Whiting's head and bruises over his body. Both Burt and Sarah Miles had come forward immediately after the discovery of the body and given detailed statements to the authorities on the preceding events. At no time did either of them make any attempt to evade justice. Both were frank and cooperative in replying to the questions from the police. Still it continued to make headlines even after a public inquest had determined Whiting's death as suicide.

The following statements were issued within a day of each other, one by Burt Reynolds and the other by MGM, who had hired attorneys to represent both Reynolds and Miles for the protection of their civil rights.

BURT REYNOLDS STATEMENT
RIO RICO INN, NOGALES, ARIZONA
SATURDAY, MARCH 3, 1973

First, I want to thank you for coming all the way out here to talk to us.

Up until now I have not talked to any member of the press or even issued a statement. I am told by some of the attorneys that this might possibly have been construed by the press as my feeling that I had something to hide. Nothing could be further from the truth, and I want to clear that situation up now.

I must say that I am very sorry that you and I are being forced to spend our time and energy on something that *rightfully* should require neither.

I am terribly sorry about the death of David Whiting. I did not know the man, except to say hello; I was not knowledgeable about his relationship to the Bolts *; I was unaware of his two previous suicide attempts or the fact that he had beaten Miss Miles only one week earlier; I was not present when he physically beat Miss Miles on the night of February tenth; I did not see the man take the pills.

More than anything else, I do not like the fact that I have been put in the position of somehow needing to explain or defend myself, when there isn't one single, logical reason in the whole world for me to be defensive or to give any explanations.

---

* Sarah Miles' husband was Robert Bolt.

My only personal involvement in this entire situation was the fact that I gave shelter for the night to a woman who had been badly beaten up by a man who later that night took an overdose of pills and killed himself. That is the total extent of my personal involvement.

And yet, for the past four or five days there have been numerous rumors and innuendoes suggesting that there was more to the death than an overdose of pills, and that important evidence was being hushed up to "protect prominent people." That is totally untrue.

You have all just read the transcript from last Tuesday's inquest, and you know that the medical examiner and the toxicologist have categorically stated that the cause of David Whiting's death was a self-administered overdose of pills and that *there was no other contributing cause of death.*

This is irrefutable, incontrovertible *proof* of what really happened that night, and it seems obvious that there is nothing more that I or anyone else can or should add to that to make it more definitive, and that nothing else about that night is relevant here except the cause of death.

I hope to God that this will be the end of any and all questions that anyone might have about the situation, as well as my involvement in it. I am very grateful to you for coming to clear the air surrounding David Whiting's death once and for all.

MGM STATEMENT
SUNDAY, MARCH 4, 1973

MGM wishes to make a statement concerning the suicide of Miss Miles' business manager, David Whiting, on February 11, 1973, in Gila Bend.

It is terribly sad that a human being's life has ended prematurely. But it is equally sad that two people who are alive are having their names and reputations dragged through the mud simply because they happen to be celebrities.

MGM has been advised by its counsel that the official medical report concerning the death of David Whiting, which was read at the inquest into the matter on Tuesday, February 27, states that the cause of his death was due to an overdose of pills and that there were no other contributing causes of his death, including the presence of a minor head wound.

And yet public talk still persists that there has been "Suppression of facts." MGM has not suppressed any facts and does not know of any facts to have been suppressed.

69

Immediately after the body of David Whiting was found, Miss Miles and Mr. Reynolds voluntarily gave full statements to the policemen who investigated the death. After the statements were made and the police investigation concluded, MGM was advised that the police were satisfied that David Whiting took his own life.

Following the police investigation, the county attorney conducted an independent investigation with the help of the State Police, which consisted of interviews with Miss Miles and Mr. Reynolds, which they voluntarily agreed to.

MGM counsel further advised that after the complete statements of Miss Miles and Mr. Reynolds and an interview of all other material witnesses as well as the medical examiner's report and the findings of the toxicologist, Mr. William Parks and Mr. Douglas Peacock of the County Attorney's Office as well as the State Police determined that it was clearly a matter of suicide and have reported this conclusion to the coroner.

MGM is confident that the police, the county attorney, and the medical examiner and toxicologist have put to rest this sad incident.

During the following weeks production continued, as the cast and crew struggled to maintain some semblance of order in the midst of the chaos that persisted. The March 6 issue of *The Phoenix Gazette* carried a story that stated, "Reynolds is a prisoner in his own room. He has had to hire a guard to keep the thrillseekers away. The telephone, which is a direct line to the motel room, is constantly ringing at all hours of the day and night." The account went on to state that Burt was having a difficult time explaining the bad publicity to his parents.

Finally, after weeks of strain, the case was declared officially closed by Gila Bend Chief of Police J. T. Cromwell, who, on March 23, said he was "ringing down the curtain" on the investigation into the death of Whiting.

During this time, the support and loving devotion of Dinah helped Burt to get through what he would always think of as an unbelievable nightmare of events.

Rushing to his side, Dinah too was besieged by reporters for a statement. "If *I* were in trouble I'd call on Burt," she told them, adding that it was natural for Sarah Miles to have called upon Burt when she needed help.

Not once was she swayed by the rumors of a romance between Burt and Sarah, a motive that the rumormongers said might have caused Whiting's outburst, since it was said that Whiting had been infatuated with Sarah. For Dinah it was a time of giving totally to her man.

And yet there were those who did not come forward with the emotional support he needed at that difficult time. Those friends, like Hal Needham, who *did* step forward became even more cherished. Somehow Hal was able to get Burt away from the local press, who were all too eager to continue exploiting the tragic death of David Whiting. Afraid that his good buddy might end up in a lot of unnecessary muck and mire, Hal stepped in, urging Burt to pack up and leave town as soon as the case was closed.

The company moved on to continue the picture at the next location. The enthusiasm and zest had gone and the film was completed in an atmosphere of residual strain. Getting back to normal was what everyone was working toward. But things were not to return to normal that easily. On March 31, Burt was hospitalized for emergency hernia surgery. The hernia was re-portedly sustained during a fight scene that had taken two days to film. Neither Burt nor Jack Warden, with whom he had staged the fight scene, had used stunt doubles. According to an April 5 release in *Variety,* "the injury was worsened when Rey-nolds was galloping his horse on four feet of snow on location in Kanab, Nebraska."

Filming was suspended while Burt recuperated at Dinah's house, where he had gone after leaving the hospital. He had signed to make a science-fiction film, *Zardoz,* for Fox, which John Boorman (*Deliverance*) was to produce and direct. But on April 30, the day after *Cat Dancing* was completed, the morn-ing issue of *Daily Variety* noted that Burt was unable to do any more work for a while. His doctor had ordered six weeks of rest.

He retreated to Jupiter.

But he was troubled. The ugly rumors persisted. There seemed to be no letup to the aftermath of that terrible day, a birthday Burt will never forget and one he no doubt would have preferred to skip, had he been given a choice. One night he decided to take his cause to his fans. While making an ap-pearance on "The Tonight Show," Burt took a deep breath and became quite serious.

"I don't lie to you," he said, looking straight out at the television audience. "This is a bunch of hockey puck they're throwing at me."

"Everyone applauded," he remembers. "I got tears in my eyes."

But not everyone was as kind or as understanding of his plight. In the June 16 issue of *Variety*, it was reported that an incident occurred while Burt was making an appearance on "The Mike Douglas Show," which was being picketed. One of the picketers shouted to Burt that he would "do anything for money, even murder." Burt was reportedly held back by associates from going after the person who had made that accusation.

Months later, in speaking with a reporter of the Gila Bend tragedy, he said, "I still haven't gotten over it."

From Jupiter he replied to rumors that he was very ill, "There's nothing mysterious about my illness. It's simple. I just collapsed from physical exhaustion. The horrendous physical and emotional strain that went with *The Man Who Loved Cat Dancing* immediately followed by surgery for a hernia.

"I got on my feet too soon after the operation, even making preparations to start *Zardoz* in Ireland." Sean Connery was to play the role instead.

Burt had acquired the great-grandson of Man O'War. In the weeks of rest at the ranch he had become better acquainted with himself, gratefully refreshed in the tranquility of his true home and the happy hours with the woman he loved. Time and rest were healing him both physically and emotionally. By the date of the premiere of *Cat Dancing* in June, Burt was well enough to attend. The United Artists Theater in Westwood (a suburb of Los Angeles) was the scene of the celebrity-laden event, a black-tie benefit for Concern for Cancer Research.

A gala party preceded by a demonstration of Indian dances and chants was enjoyed by the cast as well as the all-star turnout. But about six weeks later, Burt and MGM came to a confrontation when he protested the advertising used to promote the film.

"Burt and Sarah in the torrid love story that shocked the country," the billboards announced.

Furious, Burt threatened to sue unless the studio did something about it. He was rightfully angered by what appeared to be an attempt to exploit the incident at Gila Bend.

In the early days of his career Reynolds bore a strong resemblance to Marlon Brando.

Marriage to actress Judy Carne in 1963 lasted three years.

Wearing his "Dan August" jacket and the "look" that symbolized the police detective.

Burt's sense of humor is one of his most admired traits.

Burt and actress Miko Mayama were together for four years.

Burt and Dinah Shore were the most talked-about couple in Hollywood for many years.

Playing one of his favorite types of role, that of a football player, Burt tosses the ball on the set of Semi-Tough.

Burt and Sally Field were expected to make it to the altar, but broke up after nearly four years together.

*"I don't want to be the
next Johnny Carson,
the next Gable, the next
anything. I just want to
be Burt Reynolds."*
*Posing here with the
wax museum figure of
his character in*
Deliverance.

Enjoying some time away from the camera with Semi-Tough *co-stars*
Kris Kristofferson and Jill Clayburgh.

Sharing a joke with good pal Johnny Carson at one of the many awards parties given in Burt's honor.

A star bearing his name is placed in the starwalk on Hollywood Boulevard in an impressive ceremony.

Liza Minnelli became a good friend after co-starring with Burt in Lucky Lady *in the mid-seventies.*

Pictured in his "Dan August" role, Burt autographed this photo for the author, who first interviewed him on the set in 1970.

The studio readily complied and the wording of the new advertisement for *The Man Who Loved Cat Dancing* was changed to read: "Burt and Sarah in the torrid love story that shocked the Old West."

By the middle of summer Burt had regained his health sufficiently to proceed as star and co-producer with the taping of "The Burt Reynolds Late Show," a proposed six-segment series that was in negotiation with NBC decision-makers. Despite pessimistic comments from a number of authorities in the television industry, Burt taped four specials: "Burt Reynolds at Leavenworth," "Burt Reynolds in London," "Burt Reynolds in Nashville," and "Burt Reynolds and the Girls." The shows were aired with very little publicity, and were fairly well received by late-night viewers.

Remarkable about one of the tapings was the fact that it took place inside Leavenworth prison, where thirty-three inmates had been selected to perform on the show with Burt as emcee. Backed up by a crew of technicians, Burt arrived at the prison somewhat uneasy as to whether or not he would be able to do the job he had set out to do. Why had he chosen to film a talk-show series?

"I am not, essentially, a movie star," he modestly stated. "I am essentially a TV personality. I'll be doing what I love most of all: going out and putting myself on the line, warts and all, unrehearsed. If I could bring it off with those guys at Leavenworth then I'd know I'd made the right decision."

According to an article in the October 13, 1973, issue of *TV Guide*, "the audience responded—even to the feeblest jokes in Reynolds' monologue—like a great, electrified organism, in the longest and loudest nonviolent demonstration in the history of the Big Top."

In September, he reported for work at Georgia State Prison in Reedville, Georgia, where he was to film *The Longest Yard*, a story centered around a prison football game. Returning to complete the film on the Paramount lot in October, Burt was starting to feel like his old self again. His health had improved. He was ready to plan his next feature, and in November announced his plans to do so.

"I feel a moral obligation to Fox Studios [for bowing out of *Zardoz* when he was ill] and will probably do *W. W. and the Dixie Dancekings* as my next feature."

Despite his grueling schedule, the year was not relegated just to the pursuit of his career. From time to time a bit of levity in the form of practical jokes between Burt and his playful friends eased the tension.

One such incident occurred sometime in the latter part of the year, when Burt's friend Bert Convy hired a college marching band to serenade the sleeping couple outside Dinah's home, where they were startled into wakefulness at 3 A.M. The "event" aired on the December 23 "Tonight Show." The two are still contriving to outwit one another as they try to dream up something that will be the practical joke to end all practical jokes.

In November, when her NBC television special "Timex Presents Dinah in Search of the Ideal Man" was aired, the following free verse poem written by Dinah was an expression of her feelings:

My ideal man
Is many men; for I am many women.
He can afford the luxury of tenderness
Because he will be so innately strong.
He will need me
And he will be there and know when I need him.
We will share and he will care so much
That for once I can tell him what is in my soul and
Where I have failed
And he will not find me smaller for my failings.
He will be wise and fair
And honest with himself and me.
I will like him and
He will like me.
He will be proud of me—
Of what I am and not who I am—
For what I do for him
And for others close to me
And not for what I have done for others not so close.
He will let me be a person—
A woman—
He will let me give,
Knowing I have a need to give
And we will weave a gentle web
Of possessiveness around each other,

Not because of our insecurities
But because of our interdependence.
He will listen
And perhaps like what he hears
But if he does not like or agree—treat me as he would
A treasured friend—
A respected friend.
He may not like all those people I like—
But he'll be with them knowing
That if they have meant something to me at any time—
They are not a threat to us
But a cementing of our present and our future
Through a knowledge of our pasts.
He will know our lives did not begin the day we met.
Whoever I am—whatever he loves—
Began with and is an accumulation of people and
Experiences and living.
But he will know my day begins and ends with him—
The way I treat my friends, my helpers, my dog,
My work, my play depends
On how I feel he feels about me on that day.
We will laugh together when we are together
And separately when we are not,
Knowing that later, in delicious comfort,
We will share that laughter.
Above all he will like to be with me
And we'll need each other
Loving, touching, holding, filled with the wonder of
One independent and separate soul
Who, through some miracle, found another independent
And separate soul
Melded together
Not as one lump of indistinguishable matter
But many, myriad, exquisite facets and textures and shapes—
Joined in beauty—
A definite oneness of inseparable strength—
Balanced in stresses and tensions
Totally resistant
To structural and spiritual failure.

No one was in doubt as to who had inspired her words.

CHAPTER
TWELVE

he Longest Yard, released in September 1974, was to gross seventy million dollars.

Burt's next two films, departures from his usual roles, were not to fare nearly as well. In the annals of film history both *W. W. and the Dixie Dancekings* and the highly touted Peter Bogdanovich production of *At Long Last Love* were mere whispers in the wind.

At Long Last Love was a challenge for Burt, according to the production notes issued by 20th Century-Fox Studios. "In the film he sings, dances and reveals an adroit gift for comedy-timing absent from the screen since the heyday of Cary Grant."

Burt had expressed a long-secret dream to do a musical and was optimistic about his role of Michael Oliver Pritchard III. The film was something of a spoof of the 1930s and, while it was a gathering of many talents, critics cut it to the quick when it was released in March 1975. By that time Burt was heavily involved in other projects and, although he felt the sting of the critics, he was able to go about his business with no more than a sense of disappointment and the confidence that perhaps he would try again in the future. It seemed that filmgoers were turned off by light, frothy pictures and instead paid their money at the box office for what they considered more meaningful films. It was an era of the realistic movie.

The fan magazines were busily speculating about whether or not Burt and Dinah would become husband and wife. One reporter recalled that Burt had told her, in a pre-Dinah interview, "Marriage is in style if you have babies. I would get married if I fell in love with someone I wanted to have babies with."

That seemed to answer the question as far as she was concerned. But of course there was more to marriage than having babies, others argued. Burt and Dinah had been together for two and a half years. The relationship appeared to be as deep and satisfying as ever, and Burt seemed to be ready to commit himself to a life of pecan pie and slippers.

He often referred to the magical romance of Gable and Lombard and their brief but joyous married life. He spoke of the stages of a relationship. First came the fireworks stage, and then a gradual fading of those initial fireworks until one moved into the fourth stage, when it is possible for a romance to fizzle out. At the time, he said, he was in the third stage with Dinah and it was "really pleasant and terrific."

"I like a woman who thinks she's sexy, that's important to me. I like a woman who is vulnerable. A romanticist. Not possessive. She should be her own woman, self-sufficient."

Dinah was certainly all of that and much more.

And yet the magazines also persisted in printing stories that intimated Burt was not completely satisfied with a one-to-one relationship, that he did occasionally go out on Dinah. One such story quotes three girls as having dated Burt when he was away from Hollywood. When Burt and Bernadette Peters, who had made *Silent Movie* together, were in New York the same week, they spent an evening partying with a group of friends. It was just a play and a late supper, but the columnists made a big item of their friendly evening together.

Burt is reported to have given Dinah a $20,000 Maserati soon afterwards, but whether that was to soothe any hurt feelings she might have had because of the incident or for a special occasion was never explored. The columnists and magazine writers preferred their own hastily drawn conclusions about Burt's generous gift.

Another rumor centered on Dinah's reaction to Burt's "dates" with other women. "Whenever Dinah hears about Burt and some other girl she goes into a real blue mood. But she never takes out her hurt feelings on anybody, just herself. She gets all withdrawn and broody. And she never, never takes out her hurt feelings on Burt. She never wants him to know that she's hurt," a friend said.

Burt was heard to comment: "I've done a lot of things but I've never lied to her. I don't lie to women . . . but I do fool around. I'm very happy right now. Some of my happiest moments are when Dinah and I are at my ranch in Florida."

77

Despite Burt's comment about fooling around, the fact that he and Dinah were still close, that the relationship was on solid footing, was evident whenever they appeared together in public.

On February 14, 1974, their arrival at the Photoplay Gold Medal Awards party at the Beverly Hills Hotel was the highlight of a gala evening. Looking as cozy and happy together as ever, the two were quickly surrounded by a roomful of enthusiastic men and women, the majority of whom were in the entertainment industry. The proof of their enormous popularity was that even the press seemed to perk up and get carried away in the admiration for this special couple. They generated their own excitement just by entering a room together.

The stretch of time spent filming *At Long Last Love* was the longest period Burt had spent in his Hollywood home since his career had sent him all over the country making movies. But by the close of 1974, he was into production on *Hustle* with gorgeous Catherine Deneuve. According to a story by Roger Ebert in *The Los Angeles Times,* Burt is reported to have said the reason that the making of *Hustle* was kept rather low key was because he and Dinah were breaking up.

"The gossip columns would have had a field day, claiming that Catherine was stealing me away from the American flag. When actually it was no such thing. Dinah and I had some wonderful years, and then it ended."

It did not, however, end that abruptly.

Of Miss Deneuve, he has said, "She's a fascinating woman. All the right qualities. And she's terrifically funny. Loves to laugh. For most men it's hard to see beyond *that face.* But she has a great, bawdy sense of humor. Most men try to elegant her to death. And she hates that. You cannot take her to too rotten a place. The more rotten it is the better she likes it."

Of Burt, Catherine Deneuve has said, "He is nothing like his image. He is shy and sensitive. A very nice person."

But it was not a romantic involvement with this very beautiful, talented actress that led to the breakup of Burt and Dinah. He was quick to point out that Catherine was a woman not to be taken lightly, that she was a woman to whom one would be expected to make a commitment.

"If you made a move on Catherine, you'd better be prepared

78

for her camping right where you are. Everybody else is out. She's that kind of woman."

In her December 31 column, Marilyn Beck again reported on the romance of Burt and Dinah. This time the report was far from optimistic. "We've become like two ships that pass in the night," Burt was quoted as saying. "Her new CBS show is really hurting us. The hours she puts in trying to turn out a top, ninety-minute, daily program are killing. I come home at seven, she doesn't get there till ten, and by then I'm really bugged. And when she is home, she's just exhausted, thinking only about the next day's production. You can't do a show which demands you give so much of yourself and have anything left over to give anyone else."

Burt, the columnist continued, wanted Dinah to work a little less hard. His solution was for her "to do what every other TV headliner does, have a co-host or a supporting regular to take over some of the load. She hasn't gone along with that idea yet, though. I thought she'd relax a bit when she proved her point, when her new show turned out to be such a stunning success. But nothing's getting better."

In February, Burt reported for work in Guaymas, Mexico, for the start of filming on *Lucky Lady,* in which he starred with Liza Minnelli and Gene Hackman. The film, under the direction of Stanley Donen, was to be in production for ninety-six difficult days. Guaymas is described in the 20th Century-Fox production notes as "a drowsy seaport on the Gulf of California" whose principal industry, until the arrival of camera, crew, and cast of *Lucky Lady,* was fishing. The location had been selected for the calmness of the sea. Since a great many of the scenes in the picture were to be shot on board a small craft, it was important that the weather be predictable, the usual case in that part of the country.

It was, however, a time for the unusual. According to Manny Louis, the marine equipment consultant and former U.S. Navy man who was the film's boatmaster, "The seas in that part of the Gulf in springtime usually have winds from the south. They are placid winds causing gentle ripples, but unpredictably, on several occasions, their direction completely changed. Winds came in strong from the north. We had over five hundred people and ninety-seven boats at risk during those times."

79

During the five months of shooting, two boats, one of them a camera boat with valuable equipment on board, were lost.

The three principal players spent as much as fourteen hours a day being tossed about in their boat on the frequently rough seas. Needless to say, a great deal of Dramamine was consumed. Aboard the sixty-foot craft was a daily group of as many as fifty people plus cameras, lights, cables. After filming the sea sequences, Burt remarked, "This picture saved me seventy thousand dollars. I'd been thinking of buying a yacht."

Hackman commented that it was the hardest film he'd ever had to do in terms of physical pressure and mental strain. It was Liza who was credited with being the barometer of the unit's morale. If she was happy, the production notes state, then the crew was too. And Liza, completely happy and enjoying her co-starring role with two of Hollywood's finest, was willing to accept this grave responsibility. "I had a firm basis for being happy. I liked what I was doing. I cared about Burt and Gene. They were my friends. I felt an obligation to help them if they felt crummy."

On weekends Liza's husband, Jack Haley, Jr., would fly in on the company charter, and often, at the start of filming, Dinah would take time away from her busy schedule to visit Burt on location, as she had been doing since their romance began. One observer recalls, "She really lit up the place. She's a naturally radiant woman. She seemed very happy to be around Burt. And when she went home, she took his laundry."

But by April, columnist Joyce Haber had reported that indeed Burt and Dinah had split. Fans and friends were aghast. How could this have happened? Was there another woman involved? Why had they broken up so abruptly? Haber insisted that her source was unimpeachable, someone right on the scene in Guaymas where Burt was supposedly telling everyone that the romance was over. In addition, Ms. Haber said that she had learned that Dinah had not visited Burt for a few weeks.

In Palm Springs, where Dinah was playing in the annual Colgate–Dinah Shore Golf Tournament, she expressed surprise at the rumor when questioned by a reporter. "If we've split, it's news to me," she said.

Neither Burt nor Dinah was available for a discussion of the situation.

In the meantime in Guaymas, Burt was capturing the heart of every woman within sight of him. His appearance at a society wedding nearly incited a riot as the women guests surrounded him, vying for his attention, or perhaps the chance to touch him, perhaps even to dare a kiss.

By July 1, the film had wrapped and Burt was preparing for his next movie venture, *Gator,* to be shot in Georgia. This time he would be not only the star but, for the first time, director of the film.

"I love the South," he said.

When questioned by a journalist friend about the breakup with Dinah, Burt replied, "Dinah was the great love of my life. She is the best friend I have in the whole world and I will always love her. We're closer now in terms of friendship than we ever were. But I'm not only seeing her and she's not only seeing me. It's difficult for people to believe that she and I are still wonderful, wonderful friends. But we are."

In September, Burt left for Savannah to begin *Gator,* in which his leading lady was model Lauren Hutton. Burt had originally labeled the script "the worst thing I ever read," until he was informed that he would direct as well as star in the film about a former moonshiner turned lawyer. This chance to do what he had longed to do for so many years, direct a feature film, was the most important fact to be considered. The film was, in its way, a turning point in Burt's career, giving him that extra confidence he needed to assure himself that his ambition to be a director could be realized.

"Directing is a big responsibility and the details obsess me. Twenty years ago I told myself I'd rather direct than act and it's taken me this long. You lose your passion in acting. You make too many mistakes. Maybe that's why I make so many movies; if you don't like this one, another one's opening on Tuesday. I spent six months on *At Long Last Love,* a picture nobody saw. I enjoyed making it, I learned from it. I grew, but that's too much time out of my life."

From the set of *Gator* came rumors that Burt was not well. On the night of November 20, his arrival at the Tony Duquette Studios in Hollywood for the scheduled roasting of Hal Needham prompted a friend to observe that Burt appeared to be very tired and a little under the weather. At his side, smiling brightly and looking as lovely and happy as ever, was Dinah. As always, the arrival of this duo attracted a crowd of admirers even among the all-industry guests who were as intrigued by seeing the two together as any of their millions of fans would have been.

Also present at this important event honoring the famous stuntman were Gene Hackman and Lee Meriwether, both of whom had many wonderful comments to make about this greatly admired man who had earned the respect of Hollywood. At one time or another, Hal had been the stunt double or stunt coordinator for a number of big names in Hollywood.

Up on the podium, seated next to his pal, Burt appeared more relaxed. And as the evening progressed, with a number of celebrity guests taking their place on stage to "roast" the man of the evening, Burt seemed to grow even more relaxed. This was Hal's night, and Burt's pleasure in the tribute was as clear as the smile on his face. Over the years, the men had taken turns honoring and supporting each other at various times. It was a friendship that had endured through a great many triumphs and failures and would continue to grow even stronger as time went on.

When Hal had nearly gotten himself killed doing a dangerous stunt on *White Lightning,* it was Burt who rushed to his aid before anyone else could reach him. It was just one of the times in a career laden with danger that Burt had faced the possibility of losing a man whose friendship could never be replaced. When, during the shooting of *Gator,* Hal was to double for Burt on a scene that called for him to hang onto the outside of a pickup truck, Burt, on a strong hunch, insisted that Hal not do the shot. Hal, worried about his friend meeting the shooting schedule on his first directing assignment, insisted that they proceed.

"Just roll your cameras, here we come," he shouted as the driver put the truck into gear.

"You hurt yourself, you son-of-a-bitch, and I'll kill you," Burt retorted.

He knew what could happen. And it did. The truck made a turn and caught Hal in the shoulder, causing slight injury.

On the set of *Nickelodeon,* when Burt became ill, it was Hal who stepped in and took over. "Burt did one fight that lasted for two days. The temperature was a hundred and ten degrees. I don't know how he did it, he was so sick it was scary. He would look as white as a sheet of paper. He'd do a big routine, then go into the trailer and faint. They'd make another setup and he'd go back. That man hangs in there. He has fortitude. But it got so bad he had to go for medical help and while he was gone I jumped in and did some stuff for him."

As the new year hovered on the horizon, Burt waited optimistically for whatever it was to hold for him. Nineteen seventy-six was to be a year of complexities—new directions in his career, a new love, and a succession of high-grossing films. Along with all these wonderful promises of triumph, the year was also to bring the strain of ill health—and a deep-rooted fear that he would not live to see the rest of his dreams fulfilled.

CHAPTER
THIRTEEN

Despite the appearance of the two together at the Hal Needham Roast, it was soon very apparent to everyone that Burt and Dinah were no longer an "item." And, as Burt began to be seen around with such well-known women as Chris Evert and Tammy Wynette, even his loyal fans had to face the fact that the romance of the decade was truly over.

Tammy, who had become the most popular female country-music star, was candid about her feelings for Burt. "I just think he's the greatest person I ever met," she told reporters. "I have so much respect for him and I'd have to say he's the finest man I've ever met. Beyond a doubt."

"He's so charming and handsome. *Anybody* would be taken with Burt. But," she said hesitantly, "I just don't want to cause him any problems, or Dinah. I love Dinah. She's a very close friend and a wonderful person. I enjoy bein' with Burt Reynolds but I don't want to cause him any pain. I think his relationship with Dinah is more friendship than anything. Burt's very protective. He doesn't want to hurt anyone either. I do know that Dinah is his very closest friend. He has so much love, respect, and admiration for her. Yet it just seems that every time he's seen with anybody else, people come down on him. He doesn't deserve that because Burt is just not the kind of man to hurt."

For Christmas that year, 1975, Tammy gave Burt a classic '55 Lincoln Continental in mint condition. Burt had been looking for just such a car to add to his collection and Tammy, having heard him mention that fact on a Nashville radio show, had decided to give it to him.

"I was knocked off my feet when I looked out my window on Christmas day and saw this expensive and hard-to-find classic being driven up to my house. I was shocked by her generosity, but it was a terrific gift from a lovely lady. I find in her so many endearing qualities," Burt said in describing his relationship with the queen of country music. "She's so sensitive to people who are unimportant to her life. She has this enormous curiosity about the world and yet she talks about her lack of sophistication all the time. But Tammy's sophistication has nothing to do with what comes out of books. When you've been around the world and played for kings and queens as she has, you're as worldly as anyone."

In her autobiography, *Stand By Your Man,* Tammy wrote frankly of her relationship with Burt and the fact that they were lovers from shortly after their meeting in the fall of 1975 until a few weeks before her marriage in July 1976.

Tammy's decision to marry real estate executive Michael Tomlin was an impulse, she admitted, born out of her frustration with the fact that Burt was too involved with his career to ever take her seriously. Or any woman for that matter.

Although he sent his love and wishes for her happiness, Burt did not attend the wedding because he was hard at work on yet another film.

Tammy's marriage lasted forty-four days. After the divorce from Tomlin she continued to see Burt but the relationship soon settled into a very close friendship rather than a love affair.

The Christmas of that year, 1976, Burt gave Tammy a gift of expensive original oil paintings and a watch inscribed, *To*

Tammy, with love. Burt. By that time he was already romantically involved with Sally Field.

However, Tammy's observation that Burt needed more fun was probably right. His idea of fun at that time was far different from hers.

"He is a funny, witty, happy man. But I feel like he holds a lot inside," Tammy observed. "He isn't the person everyone thinks, the happy-go-lucky Burt Reynolds with never a problem. Burt has a lot of worries, a lot of things that bother him, a lot of obligations. He needs to have fun. He really does."

Burt found his fun in his work; he busied himself planning a number of important projects for the new year. He and Hal Needham had been talking about making a film about stuntmen. Both felt it would be a money-maker and at the same time give audiences an insight into what stunt work is all about.

By this time Burt had been proclaimed one of the top ten box-office draws. It was an exciting position, one he had worked hard to achieve. And yet it had its drawbacks too, as Burt discovered on a visit to Europe.

"There's a frightening difference between being a television actor and an occasional B-movie actor. When I was in Rome I couldn't move with the paparazzi everywhere. They were all over, like ants. Places where I used to be able to just stroll around and do what I wanted to do."

He had begun to exercise more care in interviews, curtailing some of his natural spontaneity.

"Now I want to know who's interviewing me, what kind of person they are, because I've been misquoted so much. And I've been lied to. When you like them [reporters], you give them all this stuff and then, for the sake of sensationalism, they cut you up into little pieces. You're never quite the same afterwards. You build up a little callus. I'm starting to distrust.

"I think I'm an original," he continued. "And part of why I am is that I go where others fear to tread and always give enough rope for anybody to hang me. I've stopped doing that."

But while he had begun to shy away from some of the less rewarding aspects of his own superstar status, he was not so callous that he failed to react in the manner of a typical fan upon meeting Ingrid Bergman.

"She came over to me in Rome and said she wanted to meet

me. *She* wanted to meet *me,*" he exclaimed. "I ran into a wall."

The press made a big thing of Burt's fortieth birthday on February 11, but, absorbed in work, Burt did not reflect too seriously on the subject. He had long wanted to make a movie based on Dan Jenkins' best-selling 1972 novel, *Semi-Tough,* and had taken an option on the book. But first there were other movies to make, one of which was to be under the direction of Hal Needham, who had nurtured a desire to direct for a very long time. Aware of his friend's dream, Burt agreed to star in *Smokey and the Bandit* if Hal would be allowed to direct.

There were those whose eyebrows shot up, whose noses wrinkled in disdain, at the concept of *Smokey* under the direction of a novice. Not only would Hal direct, but he had also written the original story about a daredevil trucker and his escapades. The only studio exec who was willing to take a chance on this unusual project was Ned Tanen at Universal.

Burt had come full circle. Fifteen years before, he had come to this studio under contract as a young and hopeful actor. Now he was back as a top-rated box-office attraction, a *superstar!*

It was a great feeling!

The film was to be a Rastar production. Years before, Burt had tried to persuade Ray Stark to let Hal direct another film, and failed. But the years had paid off in their faith in one another. Hal and Burt prepared to leave for the location site in Georgia.

An all-star cast including Jackie Gleason and Sally Field, who had proven herself a brilliantly talented actress with the April televising of *Sybil,* joined them in early August.

Burt was a great admirer of Sally's rending portrayal of the girl with multiple personalities. Sally was visibly nervous about making her first major film after so many popular but hardly demanding roles in the TV series "Gidget," "The Flying Nun," and "The Girl with Something Extra." Her one attempt to break into feature films, *Stay Hungry,* had not done much more than afford her the chance to act. But it had led to the opportunity to do *Sybil,* revealing the true depth of her talent. Sally was still the bubbly, rather shy, and beautiful young actress with whom a great many people all over the country had grown up over the years. She was itching to shed her "Flying Nun" image.

According to Burt: "She did *Sybil* and stuck it in their ears"—something he had been hoping to do himself for a long time, after the centerfold.

Sally had been divorced from her girlhood sweetheart, whom she had married when she was barely twenty. Things hadn't gone too well with her personal life or career for a long time. "Because I came up through television, I had a real no-no image where films were concerned," she says. "I was the all-American syrupy meaningless girl-next-door with no belly button. Just about as bland as you can get."

Feeling she was getting nowhere, Sally temporarily abandoned her career. It was a rough go.

"I had to sell my house to support my sons, Eli and Peter. It took almost three years before I got the chance to show what I could do."

Yet even with the raves following *Sybil,* Sally had not received any significant offers, until *Smokey.* She reported for work at the Georgia location a bit anxious.

"Burt was wonderful with her," a member of the cast recalls. "He took time to work with her alone because she was kind of nervous."

Burt's ability to make other actors feel at ease is well known throughout the industry. He is confident and relaxed, at least on the surface, and has a way of making the rest of the cast feel the same way. On the set of *Smokey,* this assurance was transmitted to Sally, who quickly gained confidence of her own and was soon having a grand time on a fun-packed movie. She and Burt were also growing very close in a personal way.

While *Smokey* was to be a huge financial and career success, it was also a difficult period for Burt, who was suffering from frequent bouts of unexplainable illness. He had shown the first sign of poor health while making *Nickelodeon,* but had gone almost immediately into another film despite warning signals from his overtaxed body. It was a year, he was to say later, "when I believed I might die at any moment."

He had passed a thorough physical in the fall of 1975, but there were recurring symptoms now that puzzled and worried Burt and his co-workers. His blood pressure would drop suddenly and he would pass out.

"One morning," Hal Needham remembers, "I went into the trailer and Burt looked like death warmed over."

Still, Burt was prepared to continue working. "Give me half an hour and I'll be ready," he insisted.

Afterwards, when the threat of dying was no longer present, Burt remembered that he would burst into laughter just as he was feeling worst.

"It got to the point where they would just prop me up and put on more makeup because I'd turned white. I'd think, 'Well, this is a good time to die. I have number-three Desert Tan on, and I'm nice and thin.' " And he would laugh uproariously.

But one day soon after Hal had ordered him home, deeply concerned about his friend's condition, Burt was hospitalized for what doctors thought was a heart attack.

He awoke to find himself in a ward with an intravenous needle in his arm. An elderly patient was tapping on his I.V., according to the story Burt later related to friends.

"He asked me to play cards with him. I told him I couldn't, that I was too busy dying. And he said that he was too but what did that have to do with a game of cards?"

He was so ill he wasn't sure that he could complete the film, but Hal was shooting around him while Burt checked into a Florida hospital for tests. Sally Field accompanied him.

Burt's illness was not due to a heart condition, according to test results, but once back in Los Angeles he was rushed to Cedars-Sinai Hospital complaining of chest pains. This time Burt knew he was on his way out. "I was being wheeled into an emergency room with an oxygen mask over my face. I was convinced this was the end, and in the middle of all the confusion someone rushed up and demanded my autograph. It was a crazy thing, but I sat up and obliged."

During his difficult months of illness, Burt was determined not to play the role of martyr. "I swore that I wouldn't burden anyone with my problems. But you want sympathy so desperately you practically stop strangers to tell them all about it. And you make a hundred bargains with God. But as soon as you feel better, you break them."

Upon his release from the hospital, where again he was pronounced free of heart disease, Burt flew to Hawaii for a much-needed rest. Sally was reported to have joined him there. It was obvious that these two had something going, and as time went by the romance blossomed into fodder for the eager members of the press, who missed the days of Burt and Dinah when copy was so easy to come by. Now it seemed that Burt had found another love, a woman who was as shy about revealing her private life as was Burt. Neither of them wanted to be the center of innumerable magazine and newspaper articles, but they were what everyone had been eagerly awaiting: a "coosome twosome," as one columnist put it.

In a kind of desperate attempt to put an end to the frequent attacks of illness that still persisted, Burt began to seek answers in a nonmedical area. On a talk show after his condition had finally been diagnosed as hypoglycemia, Burt amused the audience with the story of his initiation into meditation.

He had just taken a six-hour glucose tolerance test and from there had gone to the home of his teacher to receive his mantra. No one had explained that, not having eaten for so many hours and possibly being hypoglycemic, he should probably have had some nourishment and then gone home to rest.

After going through the "graduation" ceremony and receiving and chanting his mantra in the presence of his teacher, Burt drove off for home. On the way he found himself overcome with weakness. He was trembling, and the pains were beginning to hammer away at his chest. He pulled off the freeway onto the shoulder and prepared to meditate. It was what he needed now, to get calm, to still his mind leaping with anxiety and fear. Death seemed imminent.

But the mantra had vanished from his memory. Frustrated, Burt waited until the attack subsided. Once home, he went quickly for the phone to call his teacher.

"Please tell me quick, what's my mantra. I've forgotten the word," Burt said.

There was a slight pause and then the voice on the other end murmured, "Oh I can't tell you that on the phone. It's supposed to be a secret."

Finally, after much explaining, Burt was able to persuade his teacher to cooperate. "And then I heard my mantra being whispered into the receiver," he remembers.

He has never forgotten the word since, and, even after the diagnosis of hypoglycemia explained his illness, Burt continued to practice TM daily. Since stress was largely responsible for his dangerous drops in blood sugar, meditation has been of great value in helping him to relax.

By the spring of 1977, he was well enough to concentrate on

plans for the building of his new home, the filming at last of *Semi-Tough,* and his next directorial challenge, a comedy about death entitled, appropriately, *The End.*

Sally was off on location filming *Heroes* with Henry Winkler for Universal. But out of sight was decidedly not out of mind for either of them.

CHAPTER FOURTEEN

Burt had wanted to build his own home for some time and had purchased a parcel of land in the very elite section of Los Angeles known as Holmby Hills. It was a departure from his usual style and his announcement that he planned to live in the house now going up in this ultra-posh area was quite a surprise to his friends and associates.

"Burt always swore he would never live in any place that grand," a close associate remarked. But his tastes and his needs had changed over the years. Although the homes in Holmby Hills are in the million-and-a-half and upward price range, they no longer seemed to symbolize the "wrong" kind of life-style for him. He could certainly afford a more lavish home, and the seclusion of Holmby Hills suited his desire for privacy, something he needed within the four walls of home.

His films were grossing millions of dollars; he had reached the point of being able to call his own shots. Why not enjoy the rewards of his endeavors? The house took a year to complete, and the result shows the unique stamp of its owner clearly marked in the individuality of its interior. Of Spanish-style architecture, the house contains just one enormous bedroom with a mirrored ceiling. In the den there are four television sets. Burt is a confirmed TV addict, and it is not unusual for him to have all four sets going at the same time so he won't miss anything.

For some six years, writer Jerry Belson had been hoping to find someone with enough vision and professional *chutzpah* to bring a certain screenplay to life. He had failed again and again. There are very few visionaries or risk-takers in Hollywood these days. When Burt was involved in a hunt for screen properties, someone sent Belson's scenario, *The End,* to him. Teaming up with producer Lawrence Gordon, Burt set about to star in, direct, and co-produce this offbeat comedy about a man's coming to terms with his own death.

The subject was, he knew, certain to create ambiguous reactions when it was finally released in 1978. But armed with a cast of such magnitude as Sally Field, Myrna Loy, Pat O'Brien, David Steinberg, Dom DeLuise, Carl Reiner, Robby Benson, and Kristy McNichol, the film went into production. What pleased Burt most of all was getting Joanne Woodward to portray his wife in the film. Again he had come full circle.

"She helped me when I was a fresh-from-Florida, apprentice actor," he said. He had never forgotten how Joanne helped him get started by getting an agent interested in representing him.

"Burt works his tail off when he's working," Hal Needham said. "When he's involved there's no honky-tonking."

It was a labor of love, and of understanding. Having faced his own mortality, Burt was able to put a great deal of himself into this precedent-setting film. He accepted the fact that the critics would probably eat him alive, but his gut feeling that *The End* would be a hit where it counted, with the people at the box office, gave him confidence.

"Behind that false humor and false modesty is a bright man who's paid his dues," director Robert Aldrich said of Burt. "People think he's Charley Charm but that's only part of it. Burt is a strong-willed, self-centered businessman. He does what serves Burt, and he should."

Writer Jerry Belson remarked that what he liked best about having his script directed and acted by the same person was that it meant one less person to fight with, a fact of moviemaking that often creates more than a little trouble for writers.

Sally Field says of him: "Burt kept me from starving to death."

Their relationship continued to be a close one, and once again everyone was wondering whether Burt would marry again. Sally has two sons, and Burt is openly frank about his love for children. In an interview late in 1970 he told a reporter,

"I have done a lot of things. I've jumped free-fall from a plane, harpooned whales. But I've never had a son."

Burt's devotion to Sally's children was to become an important part of their relationship, a natural outgrowth of his love for her and a deep, basic need to feel part of a family unit.

Over the years he has investigated the possibility of single adoption, but has so far been unsuccessful in his attempts.

After completing *Semi-Tough* in 1977, Burt attended the May 10 opening of Burt's Place, a million-dollar restaurant-bar-disco in Atlanta. The Place is patterned after a Hollywood sound stage with sections named *Streetcar Named Desire, Showboat,* etc. All his friends were flown in for the festivities. Burt is not one to do anything in a small way.

He had given up drinking anything but low-calorie soft drinks and Perrier. He was following the diet prescribed by his doctor, and he was really feeling great. Yet despite his phenomenal success, he did not slow down his work schedule. He continued to go from one film into another, and all three films he made in 1977 went on to become box-office smashes.

Of the three, *Semi-Tough* was the one he felt gave him the edge in showing the kind of in-depth acting he is capable of. Although it was a seriocomic look at the life of a professional football player, there were moments when Burt's dramatic ability was very evident. There is an old bromide among show biz folk that anyone who plays comedy well is capable of a stellar performance in a serious role. Few people in the viewing audience understand how much genius goes into making us laugh.

The reviews of *Semi-Tough* were encouraging. One in particular seemed to capture the essence of Burt's true power as an actor.

"Burt Reynolds . . . is pitch perfect as the cock-of-the-walk captain," *New York* magazine's Molly Haskell wrote in her review in November 1977. "He can be subtle and ironic without betraying the basic simplicity of his character. . . . He is one of the most effortless romantic male stars on the screen."

Richard Schickel in *Time* said of Burt, "That pragmatic resistance to the con that has traditionally characterized the American spirit is so charmingly exemplified by Burt."

The End and *Hooper* fared poorly with the critics, who failed to understand the true meaning of *The End,* and directed their usual barbs at Burt in their comments.

"Because I am who I am, they've already got the knife out before they know what it's going to be about," he said, rather disgruntled. "And so I say I'm going to surprise them."

How did he plan to do that? By one day stunning all of Hollywood, especially the critics, by starring in a film that will fulfill an ambition.

"I'm trying very subtly and subliminally to ease myself away from the Billy Clyde Puckett image and toward Cary Grant. I may be the most unsophisticated Cary Grant in twenty years, but I'm going to get there."

To date his price per picture was a neat two million dollars, plus a hefty percentage of the gross. And he has already made a tidy sum just from residuals. But he does long to step out of the "good ol' country boy" image and into something more meaningful to him.

"I've painted myself into a corner. The good ol' boy roles and the talk shows have made me into a very well-paid personality. That's terrific. It was a very premeditated move on my part," he admits, "so I could get the clout to do what I wanted to do. Now I've got it.

"One of my ambitions is to be considered as good as anybody in town at acting dialogue by a writer like Neil Simon. And to be told 'Neil Simon is writing a script for you to direct.' That would be the highlight of my life. I have this giant audience out there that likes me, and I would like to lift its sights a little bit, out of the speeding car into the drawing room," he says, referring to the frequent car-chase scenes in his movies.

"I'm not sorry I'm bankable. It means I can get what I want. Now I can say, 'I want Glenda Jackson as a co-star, let George Segal drive the f . . . . . . car.' But I'm getting very businesslike about it. I'm putting on my producer's hat. I've got to get better scripts."

He was naturally pleased that Sally Field's career was also zooming upward. While working on *Hooper,* she had been offered a plum role as the star of *Norma Rae.* Yes, Sally was in *Hooper.* All in all she made four films with Burt: *Smokey and the Bandit, The End, Hooper,* and *Smokey and the Bandit 2.*

Although the two did not live together, they were "always together, even when we're apart," according to Burt. Both had been terribly hurt and disappointed in marriage. Both were idealists.

They shared a love of comedy, in addition to other things. And their senses of humor were entirely compatible. While attending a roast for Burt in Atlanta, Sally completely captivated the audience with her comments about Burt.

"The truth is this man is a sex maniac. The hotel here installed a take-a-number machine outside his room. I got number eighty-eight but the line moves fast."

Burt, quick on the verbal draw, countered with, "Sally, you and I have a wonderful relationship. You were privileged tonight," he gestured to the audience, "to see it end."

Nineteen seventy-eight was a year of awards. In March, Burt was honored with a star bearing his name placed in the Walk of Fame on Hollywood Boulevard. In September, he received two Gold Medal Awards from *Photoplay* magazine, whose readers had voted Burt their Favorite Male Star and the Favorite Male Sex Symbol of the year.

Shortly before starting production on his next film in New York, he was given the award for Male Star of the Year by the National Association of Theater Owners. In December, he was again nominated for a Golden Apple by the Hollywood Women's Press Club. Although work made it impossible for Burt to attend the gala luncheon at the Beverly Wilshire Hotel, he sent a wire that was read to the more than 400 guests present:

> I am honored and thrilled to be nominated again. If I should lose again, I'll still be honored and thrilled. Thank you.
>
> With love and respect,
> Burt Reynolds

He lost out to John Travolta, who was named Star of the Year for 1978.

In the jaded, dog-eat-dog world of Hollywood, there are not many who would have taken the time and effort to send such a wire. Burt had also donated two cases of fine champagne for a door prize. Incidents such as this one, or filling a leading lady's dressing room with flowers or remembering those with whom he's worked at Christmas, as well as numerous other acts of thoughtfulness, are what have made Burt so well liked within the industry.

That consideration and his sometimes bizarre sense of humor seem to carry him through life. On a taping of "The Tonight Show" with Steve Martin as guest host, Burt accepted Steve's challenge and on stage, in front of the audience, shaved off half his mustache. He had worn one for most of the previous seven years. Afterwards, Burt decided he liked being cleanshaven.

"I do look less sexy," he commented. "Now I look like I make love in the bedroom and not on the living-room floor."

In New York, where he was making *Starting Over* with Jill Clayburgh (with whom he co-starred in *Semi-Tough*) and Candice Bergen, the romance rumors began to circulate again. Sally Field, who was finishing up her role in *Beyond the Poseidon Adventure,* had stayed behind while Burt flew to New York.

A tabloid ran a story intimating that Candy and Burt had slipped away together for a romantic weekend on a friend's farm in Connecticut. Immediately the tongues began to wag and the phones began to ring as the gossip-lovers chewed over this tasty morsel of information. But a news photo of Burt and Sally together in New York a few days later put an immediate halt to the rumors of their having broken up.

During the summer he had taken Sally on a tour of the South, which he loves dearly. Although this relationship was somewhat different from the one with Dinah Shore, it had the same quality of caring and sharing. Sally, too, understood Burt.

"There are many things that Burt's audiences don't get to see: a shy, little-boy side that isn't in the scripts. He is the only movie star who didn't come from a hit play or a big movie. He just came crawling along, clutching and punching and digging his way," she said.

His career has brought him fame, fortune, and *happiness*—many actors have to sacrifice the latter for the first two. One of the rewarding aspects of his popularity was in the reaction of those attending a film seminar in the summer of 1978.

"It turned out to be a love-in," he says. "They showed six of my films from 1961 on down and the viewers were able to see my growth. Some actors are clones, they remain the same as twenty years ago. I've gotten better.

"*Deliverance* stunned them. *The End,*" he admitted, "was like having a baby. It was frightening."

He was looking ahead with optimism, planning for a future that would allow him the freedom to relax and enjoy the fruits of his success, not only in his career but in his personal life that meant so much to him.

One day he would concentrate on directing completely. But he wasn't ready for that yet. He had too many other wonderful things to experience.

And first on the list was the new film he was getting ready to make. A picture that could be the first step to the recognition that he felt had passed him by. Shortly after Thanksgiving he packed his long johns and headed east for the location of *Starting Over.*

He had begun to feel the impact of his efforts on those who count: the audience, the people who pay the price of a ticket at the box office. Their applause and acceptance was what propelled him along.

They loved him for his humor, his warmth and down-to-earth manner. They appreciated him for what he tried to bring to them on screen. He was jubilant and grateful.

But he longed for the tip of the iceberg: the chance to show "everyone" what he was really capable of on screen. He longed to make the critics sit up and take notice.

In his heart Burt was certain that one day, perhaps sooner than anyone believed, he would be able to add *that* to his credits.

What would he be doing if he gave up acting and directing?

"I would teach English literature or coach football. I love kids. I think you have a greater appreciation for children as you get older. But I'm not in any hurry to get married. You just have to be ready to get married and have children. I'm not ready."

And in the next breath he remarked that he hoped to be settled, a married man with kids, by the time he's fifty.

"I want to lead a quiet, pseudointellectual life and go out and direct a picture two times a year. You can only hold your stomach in for so many years.

"But I'm gonna be a fun old man!"

CHAPTER FIFTEEN

By mid-December, the filming of *Starting Over* was well under way in Boston, where the cast and crew had been moved from New York for exterior shots.

In the midst of a blustery winter, Burt tried not to think of the sacrifices he had made for this part. For the first time in many years and only the second time in his life, he would not be with his family at Christmas.

He pushed aside the feeling of homesickness that swept through him at the sounds and sights of the holiday season. Although they spoke on the phone every night, he and Sally had been apart for weeks while she made *Beyond the Poseidon Adventure*. She would be home for Christmas with her children.

Burt missed his girl. He made no effort to hide it from everyone connected with his new picture.

And there were career concessions as well, made because he had put so much stock into this particular role. Originally he had been scheduled to go into production on *Rough Cut* in London with Lesley-Anne Down and David Niven. But, after reading the script for *Starting Over*, Burt had followed a gut-level feeling and actively campaigned to get the part of the middle-aged man who flounders insecurely in the singles world after being dumped by his ambitious, beautiful wife.

Burt was convinced that this was the opportunity he had been waiting for, that this could convince the hard-nosed critics once and for all of his ability as an actor. He would show them that he could not only earn money at the box office but do a good job of acting; he had always been confident of that fact but somehow had never been able to fully convince the industry.

"Up until now my entire career for the most part had been based on playing a character who winks at the camera to show everyone that he's having a good time. When I make a movie, people say, 'Oh, it's just another one of those Burt Reynolds pictures.' This one will be different."

Determined to set to rest the stereotyped image of the past several years, Burt spent two hours convincing director Alan Pakula that he should cast him in the part. Robert Redford and Dustin Hoffman had been considered for the role.

Burt told himself over and over that he was perfect for the role, despite the twinges of apprehension that occasionally made him wonder if he had made the right career move.

"When we started the movie, I told Alan that people were going to say he took a hell of a chance casting me. Actually, he couldn't lose, though, because if I turned out well, he would get the credit. If I was really terrible, he could always say that the studio made him use me."

Burt was uncertain at first whether he and the director could work well together. "He's a perfectionist," he said of Pakula, "and I knew that he had some doubts about me in the part."

But, as 1978 drew to a close, the relationship between director and actor became one of mutual admiration. Giving up all his approvals (of director, cast, crew) to persuade David Merrick to delay the filming of *Rough Cut* was a concession worth making, Burt assured himself.

"There's a lot of me in this part," he admitted. Although he was certainly not the image of insecurity and shyness he was portraying, there were bits and pieces within the film with which he closely identified. "That scene in the department store where he starts to hyperventilate and his brother asks for a Valium," Burt said, "and everyone standing nearby holds a Valium out to him? Well, that actually happened to me. I was having dinner in a restaurant with friends when suddenly I couldn't catch my breath. I started to hyperventilate. I remember asking if anyone had a Valium and about thirty people responded."

Drawing upon his own experience, Burt used his acting skill to create a scene that was both funny and touching. It was to be one of the best scenes in the picture, praised by his peers and adored by moviegoers.

What very few people were aware of was that, years before, Burt had desperately wanted to try out for the lead in *One Flew over the Cuckoo's Nest.* He was convinced that he had lost the opportunity of even reading for the part because of his *image.* In Hollywood, it is all too common for the decision-makers to overlook an actor because of what he's done rather than what he is capable of doing in a role. Burt was not the first victim of a one-dimensional viewpoint.

But he was one of the most disappointed.

"I don't think that I would have played the part any better than Jack Nicholson," he commented, "but *it was not out of my range.*" The success of this film was to become his Achilles Heel; to make him chafe inwardly for years at the limited view of his acting ability with which the "decision-makers" continued to regard him.

After wrapping up *Starting Over,* Burt flew home to Jupiter to prepare for the February opening of the Burt Reynolds Dinner Theater, a $2,000,000 venture that was another dream come true for him.

Burt wanted to give something back to the industry he loves, and to his hometown as well. The Dinner Theater had been a long while in the planning stages, along with another project that Burt was equally pleased about: The Burt Reynolds Foundation for Theater Training, a nonprofit educational organization housed in the same building as the theater.

With a combined donation of $400,000 from the State University and Reynolds' personal donation of $600,000, the Burt Reynolds Chair in Professional and Regional Theater was established. It has been termed "the richest and most eminent theater chair in the United States."

Over the years Burt has personally seen to it that all graduates of the program receive whatever assistance they need. He has arranged for graduates to be auditioned for roles in television and movies. His efforts have enabled many of them to put their talents to work right after graduation. Paying his dues, as he calls it, is very important to Burt, friends are quick to point out.

But, long before he became the #1 box-office attraction,

long before he gained the wealth and popularity that he now enjoys, Burt was quietly paying his dues in the best ways he knew how. Whenever possible, he would return to his alma mater to attend a Gold & Garnet football game. He has been generous of his time *and* money. In May 1977, he attended a Hall of Fame reception. Shortly before reporting to work on *Starting Over,* Burt conducted a one-day seminar at the college.

Some four hundred students cheered and applauded the casually attired man who grinned down at them from the podium. They had come to this seminar out of curiosity as well as interest. How often did one have an opportunity to hear a lecture given by a sex symbol and superstar? A man who had once played football for their very own school?

At the close of the lecture/seminar, during which Burt was quick to joke about his own typecasting problems as well as to impart some hard truths about the business of movie-making, he had made the students into ardent Reynolds admirers and staunch devotees. Exuding that special warmth and genuine affection, Burt had imparted a sense of professional pride that inspired the four hundred members of his "class" to whistles and resounding applause. These young men and women would always regard him first as a friend, and then as a caring fellow actor—perhaps incidentally as a "star."

It was not Burt's first gesture of generosity toward his former college. In October 1974, Burt had arranged for a premiere of *The Longest Yard* as a fund-raising event for the FSU athletic department. Returning to the campus on the day of the premiere, he attended a football game with his parents and his good friend Lee Majors. At halftime Burt presented the athletic department with a check for $50,000 as his personal donation.

When he learned, via former football buddies, that his athletic trainer at FSU needed new machinery that would enable him to diagnose injuries better, Burt responded with the necessary financial assistance. During the 1978–79 academic year, he flew to Florida to make frequent spot television promotions supporting higher education in the state.

When the FSU team played the Orange Bowl in January 1979, they sported brand-new gold jackets, a gift from a former player who will always be one of the team in his heart.

100

Actor James Best remarked, "Burt is always taking everybody else's problems on his shoulders." Best, who has known Burt for as long as he's been in the business, was remembering the time when he could not find work after suffering a mild heart attack several years ago.

"I lost everything I owned. It was right after Burt found out that his television series "Hawk" was about to be canceled. He offered me five thousand dollars, but I couldn't take it because I suspected that it was probably all the money he had. But, just before the series ended, Burt managed to get me a job directing one of the last episodes. By that time no one cared, since the series was on its way out. So Burt got me a part as a villain, too. I was living in Jackson, Mississippi, because I couldn't get any other work in this town. Well, by the time Burt was making *Gator,* he had already started to get hot. It was his first directing job, and he sent for me to work with him."

That Burt never forgets is a truism understood by friends and co-workers, as well as family.

By the night of the official opening of the Burt Reynolds Dinner Theater, he was floating in a sea of contentment. His career had taken a new direction, one he felt certain would open doors that had been closed to him for too long. For the first time in a long while, he was feeling really well again. It had taken two years of abstaining from any alcoholic beverage ("I was up to a fifth of vodka a day before I got so sick"), plus a regular intake of as much as sixty milligrams of Valium, often combined with Seconal, to bring him back to health. The hypoglycemia had gone undiagnosed for so long that it had severely damaged his adrenal glands. Burt obeyed the doctor's orders to eat frequent, high-protein meals. He abstained from sweets, though he longed for a taste of his favorite dessert, chocolate mousse. For two years he had gone for regular shots of vitamin B-12 and taken antinausea pills, until his metabolism was regulated again.

His temper no longer flared up unexpectedly and for no reason, except when he was hungry and had gone too long without nourishment. "If I start to get cranky on the set," he chuckled, "someone is sure to yell 'cheese' and we break so I can get something to eat."

"I'm forever slapping a piece of chicken into his hands," Sally added, a maternal gleam in her adoring eyes.

On the opening night of the theater in early February, as he sat at a table in the cozy playhouse that bore his name, surrounded by friends from his hometown and Hollywood who had flown in for the opening, Burt applauded more vigorously than anyone when Sally took her curtain calls following her performance in *Vanities*.

Life for Burt was in full throttle.

When the play closed, he and Sally slipped away for a romantic, secluded time together on Bora Bora. Lying side by side, they lolled on the beach outside their private bungalow, concentrating on one another exclusively. They had each worked very hard in the months just past. Nineteen seventy-eight had been a productive but wearying year for both.

It was wonderful to be free of the stress of their work and the outside world. It was great to be able to unwind, if only for a week—especially since they did it together.

In March, shortly after their return from Bora Bora, Sally's film *Norma Rae* was released. The critics raved. Sally was suddenly news!

"I remember my reaction when I read the script for *Norma Rae*," Burt was to say later. "I turned to Sally and in my best presenter's voice said, 'The envelope, please.'"

A few weeks later, when Sally flew to the French Riviera for the Cannes Film Festival, where *Norma Rae* was in competition, she left Burt in charge of her sons, Peter, then nine, and Eli, who was six.

Columnist Marilyn Beck had speculated that Burt and Sally would soon be walking down the aisle. Burt admitted as much, but he had also added again, "We're both scared to death of marriage. Each of us has failed once at it and that's a problem.

"There are times when I feel ready and I say, 'Okay, let's do it.' I feel certain that I can handle marriage. Then Sally will be the one to suggest that we wait. She'll admit that *she's* afraid. When she's ready, I'm the one who's terrified."

They had been together three years, mostly on weekends, when Sally would move into Burt's house. They frequently planned outings with the boys. Burt's affection for them was

102

obvious. Still, there were hurdles to overcome. His innate sensitivity made him very much aware of the difficulties that marriage might create for all concerned.

"I've been with Sally for three years, and it's been wonderful," he said in an interview. "I like being with her in any situation, good, bad, or indifferent. I just like being around her. She's tough, gritty, and she's got this great sense of humor. She gets prettier every day, not just to me but to other people who see how she's blossomed. Not only in her looks but in her acting. She's really blossomed as an actress. I've seen it all happen. I've been there watching. It's exciting to be in on that kind of metamorphosis.

"Sally's always been a very gifted actress. But these past few years she's gone from a television actress to being in the same league as a Jill Clayburgh and Jane Fonda. And she's gone from girl to full-blossomed woman."

Sally openly gave Burt credit for many of the changes in her, especially in her appearance. And she was quick to point out how his faith in her had given her the courage to forge ahead as an actress.

"Without his help I would have had a hard time surviving. I was so vulnerable when we first met, but I had vowed never to show it. So I went around talking like a truck driver, swearing more than any living human. I thought this would impress people with the fact that I was a real brassy chick.

"It was Burt who quietly took me aside and told me that I shouldn't act that way, that it was dumb. I started crying, and he just held me, explaining how I was diminishing my power as a woman because when a woman talks like that, men don't really listen. They just walk away and say, 'Did you hear the mouth on that girl?'

"It took a while, but I stopped using four-letter words and started acting like what I am, a woman. Vulnerable but nice, a nice person to be around.

"Burt was only the second person I ever really dated. I went with my ex-husband Steve all through high school up until we married. I could hardly believe that a man like Burt, so sophisticated, so much together with his own life and career, could actually find me attractive. I had always thought a woman had

103

to have long, painted fingernails and high cheekbones, that sort of thing, in order to make a man like Burt pay attention. I even dressed like the part or the way I thought was right for the image I was trying to project. I'd always been afraid to dress simply, so I hid behind a lot of clothes. Overdressing."

Gradually, with Burt's encouragement, she began to dress more sophisticatedly, although she frankly admitted that she preferred the tomboy look. "I'm giving it the old try," she quipped, referring to the sleek, simple dresses she had added to her wardrobe at Burt's urging.

He had also influenced changes in her career, not all of which turned out to be right, according to Burt.

"I do give her career advice. I asked Sally to get a better business manager, and I convinced her to get a bigger agent. She went with William Morris. They handle the world. But," he added ruefully, "I also was the one who talked her into doing *Beyond the Poseidon Adventure,* the worst acting experience she's ever had. She hated every minute of it. Sally's stubborn about her career, and she didn't want to do it, especially after *Norma Rae.* But they offered her a lot of money for *Poseidon,* and I thought it was a good idea to do a commercial picture. That way she could say she was not only an artistic success but a commercial one as well."

Of course, neither of them could foresee the impact Sally's performance in *Norma Rae* would have on the critics and the public.

If Sally harbored any anger at Burt for persuading her to do *Poseidon,* it was not evident. With two young sons to raise, the money had come in very handy.

"I've found that it takes about three years to find out about somebody, and then you come to grips with a lot of things," Burt said.

"When an unmarried man gets to be forty in this town, he's supposed to be either a homosexual or a heterosexual who either *wants to be alone,* is *a womanizer,* or is *a very selfish man.* The category that is left out completely is the one where the guy wants to share everything with someone special, but he also wants to allow that person to have freedom and a life of her own."

Burt's pride in Sally when she was presented with the Best Actress Award in Cannes was what prompted him to release her from her commitment to appear in the sequel to *Smokey and the Bandit.*

"No one should take a backward step," he stated. "After *Norma Rae* she should do only important things."

While Sally had been at the film festival, Burt had concentrated on her two sons. He had planned a round of activities for the three of them in his determination to learn whether or not he could really handle the role of stepfather, if he and Sally did get married.

"I'm having a slumber party for them and their friends," he said. "And I've arranged to take them to a private screening at the studio. We're going on a picnic and we're having a ball game.

"I really adore Peter and Eli," he said, "and I think they like me. But marriage is a major decision. I don't want to get married and not be able to make it work. I don't want to screw up the lives of those kids. Sally is a very strong woman, and she's very career-minded. She's not an easy lady to live with, and I'm not an easy man to live with either."

The matter of Sally's two sons was one to consider very carefully. "I had to make them see that I wasn't just a guy who wanted to be their mother's husband, that I had no intention of taking her away from them.

"When I do decide to get married, it'll happen just like that," he added, snapping his fingers. "No one will know about it beforehand. This is the best time of my life and I don't think I should live it alone. It's no good looking at the Grand Canyon by yourself.

"It's better to have a kid to share it with, or a wife, or somebody permanent and fantastic. I'm almost certain that it will happen in the next two years, and odds are that it'll be Sally. But, if I don't marry in two years, I'll stay a bachelor and adopt."

Friends speculating on the relationship felt that it had reached the point where it was marriage or nothing. It was the point at which Burt usually exited a relationship.

But where in prior years he had avoided discussing his relationship with Sally with the press, Burt was now open about his ambiguous feelings and the fate of their relationship. "Who knows, by the time this is published," he told a reporter, "Sally and I may have broken up."

He was open about other things too, admitting with good-humored candor that he had begun a series of hair transplants to the tune of $8,000. "For years I was under the impression, the illusion, that people didn't know I wore a hairpiece. A lot of them look like golf divots, but mine didn't. I thought they looked very natural, but I really got tired of bothering with all that glue and the mess that I had to deal with. And, frankly, I wanted to look better."

He had also decided to grow his mustache back and was striving to maintain a trim figure.

"I junk out on pasta once a month. I live for the day when I can gorge on linguini, lasagna. You know, weight is one of the greatest killers when you're past forty."

When *Sunday Woman* reported that Burt had given Sally a $40,000 mink coat, and that he had also given Candice Bergen a $15,000 bracelet, a reporter questioned Sally again about the rumors of romance between Burt and Candy. Sally just shrugged. "I guess I caught Burt with his hand in the cookie jar, but the fact is that when they passed out jealousy, they seem to have skipped me.

"You can't rule a man like Burt. Other women are not threats to me. I know what our relationship is and I trust that."

What was the relationship and how did it manage to survive all the pitfalls that could have sabotaged it?

"What Burt and I have together is more than a quick fling in the hay. We both feel that you don't throw your life away on a momentary sensation," Sally explained. "I never want to be the kind of woman who tells her man that he can't be friends with other women. Besides, I know he's not a womanizer. Maybe in his twenties, but not now."

Burt echoed her statement with one of his own. "I'm a notorious flirt, and very often I say outrageous things to women because it's sometimes the only way to get out of a situation that could get sticky," he commented on the capricious, devil-may-care image he often projects for the public though he never flirts with other women when he's on a date. "They don't think of me as a man who would avoid going into a singles bar due to out-and-out fear. Yet the fact is, that's the truth about me. I would be petrified. I'm not even good at making the first approach unless I do it as a kind of macho gag. I couldn't face the humiliation of possible rejection. I find it [the singles bar scene] all very distasteful."

In fact, he is an incurable romantic by his own admission. "I like meeting someone by chance. Maybe sitting next to her on a plane or across the room at a party."

That ingrained romanticism accounted for the games he and Sally played to keep the relationship revved up.

"Never underestimate the value of surprise," he advised. "You need to do crazy things to liven up the relationship, to keep it from going stale. Like maybe the woman knocks on the door and the man answers pretending he doesn't know her. Then she has to introduce herself and they go through this whole bit of getting acquainted. Or maybe the man comes home and the woman is wearing nothing but an apron.

"Sally and I usually find a play that we can act out and sometimes we'll get really crazy inventing dialogue, saying outrageous things within the characters of whatever play we're acting out, even *Macbeth.*

But there was also the serious aspect of a one-to-one relationship, as Sally explained:

"One person feeds off of the strength of the other in a good relationship. Each fills in the weaknesses of the other person. If you're hurting . . . you need to be able to come to the person in your life and say that you hurt. And you need to be comforted. But the other person can never be someone who *takes care of you.* You have to have your own life. Your mate should never feel that he is what keeps you going."

"I've reached the stage," Burt said with an edge in his tone, "when I don't want to read about the two of us anymore. It's just not fair for Sally to pick up a magazine and read about how Burt has decided to get married, or Burt doesn't think it's right for them to live together because he's old-fashioned."

He was fiercely protective of Sally and plainly fed up with those who seemed to find so much of importance in his personal life.

"I'm no different from anyone else," he claimed. "I go to the bathroom. I get sick. I get angry. I cry when I'm watching a sad movie."

It was an ambiguous position he found himself in. Part of him longed for anonymity, so he could go about his life in private. Yet, another part longed for recognition, enjoying the adulation that occasionally overwhelmed him. Success bred its own brand of monster, and he was willing to accept its price, though he couldn't help feeling irritated now and then.

When a writer asked why Burt thought his films were so successful at the box office, he replied, "I think it's because I have the ability to make people happy. And to make them like me. In my pictures, I enjoy playing this character who's not quite all there, who steps down from his truck and scrapes the manure off his boots. The guy who's always fighting for his dignity. He's antiestablishment, he's funny, and he's somebody for audiences to cheer for. A kind of hero."

In April, Sally and Burt appeared together in the Burt Reynolds Dinner Theater production of *The Rainmaker*. Burt played the lead and directed the play as well. It was Burt's first appearance on stage in his own theater, and he was, by his own description, "a basket case." While the audience waited a bit impatiently for the curtain to come up on the first act, Burt tried to conceal his nervousness. Those people out there had paid $18.95 for a steak dinner *and* to see him in a play. This was his turf. The audience would be expecting even more than usual from his performance.

Backstage, he held Sally in his arms in a long embrace, as though to draw some measure of reassurance from her. Sally's fingers trailed gently over the lines that creased his forehead with worry. They kissed.

"Break a leg, kid," he whispered as she took a deep breath, preparing to walk out onstage.

The audience cheered as she stepped in front of the footlights. Later, when Burt made his first onstage appearance, they went wild, applauding even before he spoke his first line. When they played their first love scene, a hush fell across the room. As Burt kissed Sally with gentle sweetness, an audible sigh and a few delighted giggles were heard.

Clearly these two had captivated the entire world with their love. The play was a sellout, yet the Palm Beach paper panned Burt's debut. He was naturally upset. After all, he had won an award years before for that very role. He offered an explanation, perhaps more for his own satisfaction than for anyone else's. "When you act and direct, something has to be sacrificed. Usually it's your performance. *I* may not be up to par, but I'm sure proud of the rest of the cast."

They were very happy together at the ranch, strolling hand in hand over the grounds, horseback riding at dawn, visiting with Burt's parents in the main house.

Each evening before showtime, Sally prepared a healthful dinner for Burt. "He's real bad in the kitchen," Sally admitted, laughing.

While she did the laundry or busied herself with other domestic chores relating to his comfort, Burt read. He is a voracious reader, eagerly devouring information, savoring whatever he can on subjects that interest him.

"He reads a lot of biographies of people in the business and a lot of screenplays, too. But mostly he reads anything he can get his hands on," Sally explained.

He would discuss his reading with Sally while she cooked breakfast. The scene was definitely one of domestic contentment.

Sally recalled her first impression of Burt. "I could see that in many ways he was kind of sad. Emotionally, everyone was taking chunks out of him, just eating him up. And he was so sick. He just kept giving pieces of himself to people because he couldn't say, 'No, go away from me.' These were people who called themselves friends, and it really hurt me to see it happening to such a really wonderful man."

Sally was protective of Burt. She had been from the very first, when he had looked into her eyes and said, "I think I'm ready to fall in love."

She had been his close and loving ally ever since, often standing between him and those she felt took advantage of his inability to say no when necessary.

"You have to know when to go home, lock the doors, turn off the phones, and refurbish yourself. I went through that same thing when I was making 'The Flying Nun.' It got so bad pretty soon there wasn't anything left of me to give.

"Burt just wouldn't look after himself, love himself enough to learn to say no, so I started doing it for him. I became his Joan of Arc."

Yet, his ability to charm, his innate ease with people, was one of the attributes Sally most adored in Burt. "He has the ability to have lots of friends. I don't. He can get up in front of a crowd at an award ceremony or something and be as funny as a stand-up comic and do it all extemporaneously. I get the thrill of watching him, and I sit there with my heart beating fast, as if it was me up there. When the crowd laughs at something Burt says, I just about fall out of my chair with pride in him. I want to stand up and yell, 'See that person, he likes *me.*' "

Each was giving to the other in the area he or she needed. "Fitting together like puzzle pieces," as Sally once commented.

"Actually, we're very much alike. No one would think that to look at us, at our public image," Sally explained. "But we understand each other. He knows what I feel when I work. I'm a crazed person. Burt doesn't try to pull on me. He understands because he knows what it's like to be in love with your work. I think he likes the fact that I'm a never-say-die person. I'm a real endurance expert. I'm just not going to buckle under to anything."

And in a more candid moment she gave some insight into the real Burt, the man she adored. "He's got this very insecure side. He'll start saying things like 'I don't deserve you. I don't deserve this good feeling. I'm going to lose you.' When we were in rehearsal for *The Rainmaker,* there were so many things coming at him at once. He told me that he needed my strength. 'I want you to step in my footsteps. I want you to touch me all day long.'

"So all day long I was just all over him, kissing him about thirty thousand times. What it did was make him laugh, and that was good for him. It made him forget the pressures when he laughed. But it takes time for two people to feel free enough to do things like that."

She admitted to ambiguous feelings about this very deep, meaningful relationship. And perhaps it was then that the first indication of a breakup might have been given.

"I'm really old-fashioned. I believe that when you make a

commitment like marriage, it means that you cannot just pack a bag and leave, because it involves too much baloney like signing papers, losing half your money. Marriage is a commitment. Without it, it's too convenient to pack your bag and leave. That might work for two adults who are mature enough to handle it. But not for kids. They don't understand the confusion of what's going on.

"I don't want to put my boys through anything like that. You have to build a relationship with children. You can't just throw one at them. If and when I do get married again, it will have to be with my children's consent.

"They're crazy about Burt. But he's spent most of his life without children. I can't just thrust them at him and say, 'Here—love them.' You can have instant family, but instant love is very harmful.

"I'll always be independent and Burt knows that about me. It's one of the things he likes about me. It's also one of the things that scares him. I want my life to be right for me. I want a solid home life for my kids. I guess I want Ozzie and Harriet. Burt knows that I'll be willing to walk away if something isn't right."

A year later she was to do just that.

CHAPTER SIXTEEN

When he was invited to speak before a group of theater arts students at Harvard in February 1979, Burt could hardly contain the sense of pride and pleasure he felt. But, being Burt, he also could not resist a bit of flippancy when he was questioned about the experience by a reporter afterwards. "They were hoping for a Stanley Kubrick, and instead they got this schmuck actor with a cowboy hat. But when we were through we felt a mutual respect."

Burt had always regretted having to quit college. He had given a great deal of thought to how he could complete the two years he lacked to earn his degree. Unknown to anyone but the dean and professors at Florida State and a few close associates of his, Burt began to study for his bachelor's degree. Shortly before his appearance in *The Rainmaker* at the dinner theater in Jupiter, he had taken his first final, in American history. He was jubilant to find that he had earned an A in the class.

Although his intentions were good, his busy schedule made it almost impossible to pursue his studies on any but a hit-and-miss basis. Nevertheless, he did make the effort.

While Sally made the rounds of the talk-show circuit, promoting *Norma Rae,* Burt spent his time conferring with Hal Needham on the sequel to *Smokey and the Bandit.* Sally had convinced Burt that she should reprise her role as Frog and, reluctantly, he had agreed. He still felt that her talent should be directed into other areas. But as the months went by, the offers that should have come Sally's way failed to do so. She was still the sole support of two young sons. A part in *Smokey and the Bandit 2* meant earning the money she needed to keep her household in good order.

After some deliberation, Burt decided to change the location of the film from Europe to Florida and Georgia. He had won the wholehearted cooperation of the governor of Florida, and eventually was to win public recognition for putting his home state on the filmmaking map and providing hundreds of jobs for the residents.

While Hal, who was to direct the picture, attended to the necessary tasks of assembling cast, crew, etc., Burt prepared to leave for England and the filming of *Rough Cut* at last.

Having been delayed for several months, the picture was to be plagued by one annoyance after another. Even the first meeting between Burt and his gorgeous co-star Lesley-Anne Down began on a somewhat awkward footing.

Lesley-Anne and her agent, visiting the United States, had arranged to meet Burt at his home in Holmby Hills prior to the start of production. But when they arrived at the entrance, guarded by the tall wrought-iron gates that were securely locked, they could find no way to announce their arrival, nor to open the gates so they could drive up to the house.

112

"There just wasn't any way of opening it," Lesley-Anne later told a friend, "so we just stood there like idiots wondering what to do."

Fortunately, before tempers could flare, a chauffeur-driven car pulled up alongside them. A man stepped out, smiling as he led them to the secret compartment behind which was a phone with a direct line to the house. He waved his hand, smiled again, and wordlessly drove off in his limousine.

Once inside the house, Lesley-Anne hit it off very well with Burt. She was impressed by his warmth and hospitality as he gave her a guided tour of the ten rooms, and was amused by the tanks of fish in his bedroom. He expressed delight at the prospect of working with her, told her how lovely she was, and in general charmed the accent off her.

In July they met again on the set of *Rough Cut* at Pinewood Studios in London.

Burt had once stated, "As a youngster I was made to play football, basketball, baseball. I was this guy with a lot of letters on my sweater. But inside of me was somebody I thought was really funny."

In *Rough Cut* he was to play a debonair ex-thief, a role as close to a Cary Grant part as Burt had ever come. He had always aspired to emulate the wit, sophistication, and debonair manner of Cary Grant in films. To have the opportunity to play such a role was a fantasy come true. Burt hoped that his ability before the camera would meet his expectations.

They were to be the most difficult months of filming he had ever experienced.

From the very start, the set was tense with an undercurrent of impatience and uncertainty. Because he had given up his approvals, Burt could say nothing when director Donald Siegel was replaced by an English director. For the first few weeks the cast dealt with one new director after another while efforts were made to persuade Siegel to return to his original job. Production went slowly, often not at all, as writers too were replaced. Scenes that had been shot once had to be reshot as dialogue was rewritten. The film would take five months to complete. Tempers were barely held in check while the cast and crew journeyed wearily to location sites that included Holland and Hawaii as well as Britain.

113

Burt managed to retain his professionalism despite the provocation to do otherwise. He was pleased to be appearing in a film with David Niven, an actor he had long admired. He was enjoying the couturier-styled clothes that he wore in his role as Jack Rhodes, a gentleman thief reminiscent of Cary Grant in *To Catch a Thief.* Through it all he looked forward to the release of *Starting Over* and to the reviews that he felt confident would justify the sacrifices.

Don Siegel was reinstated, and for a while the production on *Rough Cut* went smoothly. But the wet and chilly weather was something Burt could not get accustomed to, and he mentally hurried the weeks away thinking of the return to Jupiter and the filming of *Smokey and the Bandit 2.*

Sally's arrival for a short stay was one of the two bright spots of the entire five months. The other occurred in late September and early October when the reviews of *Starting Over* were released.

One in particular pleased him because it echoed a hope that he had long cherished. ". . . Reynolds has been cautiously feeling his way toward exactly this kind of different, dynamic role. He delivers a knockout performance, one which may garner him a well-deserved and long overdue Oscar nomination."

Another favorite stated, ". . . this is proof positive that Reynolds has more in him than macho. The Reynolds we see here possesses quite a flair for romantic comedy. . . ."

Jubilant, Burt arranged a screening of the picture for the cast and crew in London. They were enthusiastic in their response.

In November, after what they thought was a final wrap, the unit dispersed. Burt was relieved to be basking in the warmth of the Florida sunshine and the love of his family once again.

Nineteen seventy-nine was to be a year of more awards.

Eight thousand motion-picture exhibitors voted him the Star of the Year at their annual National Association of Theater Owners dinner. Atlanta's Variety Club named him Entertainer of the Year (Man of the Year). The award that touched him most was that of Florida Ambassador of the Arts, bestowed by the Secretary of the State of Florida, George Firestone, in recognition of Burt's part in bringing cultural recognition to the state.

114

He was also named Number One Box Office Attraction in America, and was given People's Choice Awards as both favorite all-around entertainer and favorite actor.

His career continued to zoom. But there was also disappointment, namely what did not happen despite the high hopes he had put into *Starting Over.*

"I thought that my career would change, that it would turn around immeasurably after the picture was released. But it didn't. I hoped that because of the critical success of *Starting Over* I would be offered similar roles. I wasn't. I can't see over the top of the scripts on my desk. But they're all the same as *Smokey and the Bandit,*" he sighed.

Midway through the filming of the sequel to *Smokey,* Burt had to fly to Miami for some additional shooting on *Rough Cut.* Three endings to the film had been shot in Hawaii. Now a fourth and final ending was to be filmed aboard a yacht in Key Biscayne. At last this film that had been a thorn in Burt's side from the very start was completed.

When the Oscar nominations were announced in February and Sally was listed as a nominee, the least surprised person was Burt. He was overjoyed. However, he couldn't help feeling a bit dejected about the fact that both Candice Bergen and Jill Clayburgh, with whom he had co-starred in *Starting Over,* were nominated while he had been completely ignored.

He was Number One at the box office, the reviews had praised his performance, his films made millions; but the industry failed to recognize him for what he really was: a very talented actor.

"If I want to be up for an Academy Award," he commented rather tersely, "I'm either going to have to play a tour de force of some kind or have a tracheotomy just before nominations."

He could make jokes about it, but the disappointment was deep and it hurt.

"When *Rough Cut* was first shown," he said, "the president of Paramount, the director of the film, *and* my personal manager each called me to say how fantastic Lesley-Anne Down was, and how beautiful. Nobody thought to mention me. I'm like a basketball player who's great at assists but can't score."

He continued to forge ahead despite disappointment and

even disillusionment. One day he expects to add an Oscar to his other awards. He has set aside a room in his house to display them.

"It's in my plan," he confided. "I've done everything else I've set out to do. All of my fantasies have come true, from the one about playing pro football to acting and directing. Within five years I'll have accomplished all that I want as an actor. I'll have gotten that special script—my *Cuckoo's Nest*. After that I'll move into directing, producing, and writing."

Meanwhile he was trying to head off the rumors that he and Sally were calling *fini* to their romance. The fact that they truly loved one another could not be denied. But neither could the fact that something had begun to unravel in the relationship. The press continued to speculate on the how and why.

"They're trying to work it out," friends insisted. "There are things that need to be settled between them, but they're still very much in love."

On the set of *Smokey and the Bandit 2,* the most talked-about couple in the country went calmly and professionally about their business—making a picture. Away from the camera they were as close and caring as always, despite rumors to the contrary.

"I really like to work. I'm sorry that I feel that way," Burt said in an interview. "Sally's sorry too because she hates to see me this tired. But I like to work and when this picture is over, I'll go and do some other picture."

Still he found time to do something special and very thoughtful for his girl.

While showing singer Anne Murray around his dinner theater one day in March, Burt was suddenly inspired with what he thought was a terrific idea. Reaching for a phone, he quickly dialed a number, whispering to Anne to "please sing something." Bewildered but intrigued, she burst into a rendition of her 1979 Grammy-winning tune, "You Needed Me." Burt held the mouthpiece up to her, but midway through the lyrics an excited feminine voice broke in. "Anne Murray," Sally Field exclaimed. "You're one of my very favorite singers."

The two women had never met, but each had been a long-time admirer of the other. Burt had impulsively decided that this was as good a time as any for them to get acquainted, so he had simply called Sally on the phone.

Between making movies, Burt found time to direct or star in productions at the dinner theater. He was like a top in perpetual motion, always spinning.

Week after week the tabloids and columnists predicted the breakup of Sally and Burt. Yet they continued to be seen together in public, apparently still very happy.

Until the night of the Academy Awards.

The rumors flew thick and plentiful when Sally arrived, looking happy and excited in a white dress, escorted by David Steinberg and his wife. Burt was nowhere in sight.

Burt and David were longtime friends. It was not difficult for Burt's other close friends to understand why David was escorting Sally to the awards. But the speculation continued. Everyone seemed to have an "inside" tip as to why Sally was not accompanied to this very special event in her life by the man with whom she had shared so much for four years.

"It's over. Didn't I tell you?" the gossipmongers clucked.

"Burt probably didn't want to intrude on Sally's big night. It's just like him to let her have the spotlight," a friend insisted.

Sally's acceptance speech, in which she mentioned a host of people who were important to her, but not Burt, only served to heighten the rumors of trouble in paradise.

In a candid interview with Barbara Walters some time later that year, Burt admitted that he had offered to escort Sally, but she had turned him down. "It was her choice to go without me. It wasn't mine. I asked to go with her to the Awards."

The romance had definitely hit shaky ground. Every now and then the report that they had gotten back together would surface.

"I'm either very much with him," Sally admitted, "or it's one of those times when I don't even want to see his face in a magazine around the house. There is no in-between and it's all very confusing."

Taking solace in his work, Burt continued with his long-range plan by first setting up a two-year partnership with David Steinberg in a production company that included a deal to make specials for ABC.

117

"It's very hard for me to say this out loud, but I don't have anything else that makes me feel better than work," Burt said in an interview.

Later on a talk show he was heard to comment, almost under his breath, "She [Sally] is busy with her career." It was not said in bitterness, but in resignation. He has always displayed pride and admiration for Sally. He was even prouder and more pleased for her when she won an Academy Award. But there was an undercurrent of sadness that only those close to Burt appeared to detect.

Nevertheless, he launched his next project, a film about a man who has reached middle age unmarried and wants to have a son. *Paternity* was a joint venture with Steinberg directing. With the script approved, location sites set, and everything ready to roll in a month's time, Burt signed up for a leisurely cruise.

Along came an offer he couldn't refuse: $5,000,000 for less than three weeks' work on a film, plus a good share of the profits. It was an unprecedented offer. Burt accepted without hesitation. Leisure has never been his strong suit anyway. Astonished but grateful for the fortune offered him, Burt donated $1,000,000 of the money he was paid for *Cannonball Run* to the Florida State University Theater.

The film was to be deemed one of the dogs of 1981, but by that time Burt had run, hysterical with glee, all the way to the bank. He was beginning to develop the thick hide necessary to avoid the pain of the constant barbs from critics. Only occasionally did one overlook his "Tonight Show" image and get into the nitty-gritty of the actor.

On April 30 Burt stood before an audience of two thousand in the Ackerman Grand Ballroom on the UCLA campus to accept the Charles Chaplin Award.

"In recognition of your outstanding contribution in the art of film, thereby enriching the lives of people all over the world" read the full-page ad in *The Hollywood Reporter* offering the congratulations of Paramount Pictures.

"People criticize me for not doing films such as *Coming Home,* but they're not offering them to me," he said in his acceptance speech, adding humbly, "This award came at the right time in my life, when I needed it. People think what I do is real easy because it looks easy."

If the critics wouldn't relent, the public and the movie-makers were generous with their approval. Burt has continued to win award after award.

One that was especially meaningful was that of Number One Fantasy Father voted by the readers of *Seventeen* magazine in 1980.

"Maybe they thought I'd be fair and impartial. Maybe they were looking for a friend. It's hard to figure out why they picked me," he said when notified of the award.

But there was a note of pride in his voice, a gleam of joy in his eyes at this very special honor.

CHAPTER SEVENTEEN

Burt was looking to a future time when he could remain behind the cameras. His experiences as a director, starting with *Gator*, had convinced him that this was where he wanted to concentrate his efforts, that he wanted eventually to phase out acting.

He had developed a directing style that not only pleased audiences but had won him great admiration from his fellow actors and film crews. The latter can be the most severe of critics, as anyone in the movie business will attest.

"Very few directors today have any grasp of, or communication with, the script *or* the actors. They're mostly mechanics. You can learn the camera, you can learn how to be a mechanic. All it takes is the time, but you may never learn how to talk to an actor. In the final analysis, the only thing that matters is getting the very best performance out of an actor. Some have to be yelled at, others need to be sweet-talked, some have to be lied to. Some actually require a cattle prod to get them going. What's important as a director is to be able to get each one to reach down inside, way down, and get the best possible performance he's able to give.

"Acting is such a personal thing. You have to be able to help when it's a bad day and the actor just doesn't feel like acting. It takes somebody who understands the temperament of these people. I think if I have any gift, I have that ability. I've done with actors what I always wanted other directors to do with me."

"When he's not acting, he's happiest and most relaxed working with other actors as a director," observes an associate.

Loyalty, understanding, and vulnerability are qualities admired most by Burt in another man. They are the same qualities others admire in him. "He's the most decent, honorable, down-to-earth and caring, sensitive person I've ever worked with. No one else can touch him," a production assistant commented.

"There are all sides to Burt. His humanity, his humor. His sexuality is in there someplace, too. But you just think of him as a good friend," says actor-comedian Dom DeLuise, who has worked with Burt in five films.

His reputation for loyalty extends to those who have been on his work team dating back to his days on "Riverboat." "I've had the same agent for eighteen years, the same business manager for more than a dozen years. The makeup man and I have done fifteen pictures together."

They are his family and they are good friends. But the working arrangement does not necessarily spill over into his personal life.

"They come and do their jobs, and they complain more than anybody I know," he chuckles. "But when we wrap for the day, they go home. I don't see them socially unless *they* want to see me.

"When I go on the set at the start of a picture, I make a nest for myself. I make jokes and try to get comfortable. When I'm doing comedy, I like to get into a rhythm. I begin working in that same rhythm with the crew first. Once I get them laughing, I know it's working because they're a very tough audience. Sometimes people on the outside who don't know my way of doing things criticize me for wasting time or screwing around, not doing my lines. But I am actually preparing for what's coming up in a scene."

Burt has devoted much of his free time to the dinner theater in Florida. "He tries to see one performance of every show," the producer, Karen Poindexter, has said. Whenever possible he has directed and/or acted in the theater's productions.

"Probably some of my best moments have been on stage," he recalls.

"I think when I did *Same Time, Next Year* [with Carol Burnett] it was the best thing I'd ever done. That's *my* opinion. I felt very real. The comedy was crisp and in that one dramatic scene when I had to talk about the death of my son, I cried every night that I did it. More important, I made the audience cry. Sometimes even Carol."

Asked about his method, he replied thoughtfully, "I use emotional recall just like the best Actors Studio actors do. I'll do anything to make a scene work—to connect. I teach acting at the Playhouse. We have an intern program there. What do I teach?

"I teach *listen*. Moment to moment. The toughest thing in the world to teach an actor to do is to listen. So that's the first thing I teach the kids."

Veteran actor Pat O'Brien was somewhat apprehensive when he reported for work in *The End* under the direction of Burt Reynolds. But later he had glowing praise for Burt's ability as a director.

"It was a complete revelation. I knew Burt, but I did not know the extent of his directorial ability. He has a very inventive mind and he never raises his voice. He's kind. If he had any suggestions, he would call you in back of the camera and make them very quietly. It was always most instructive.

"I marveled every day watching him. He had so many different types of personalities to direct: young people, middle-aged, and the old codgers like me. I've never had an experience quite like it."

In late spring, 1980, when Burt was announced as the male lead in Universal Pictures' production of the musical *The Best Little Whorehouse in Texas,* the rumormongers went all out. Dolly Parton, who was to be his leading lady in the film, was asked how she felt about doing love scenes with Burt, who had a reputation for dallying with his leading ladies.

Her reply was succinct. "If I was single, I would be really

looking forward to the love scenes in the movie. But I'm not single . . . and," she laughed, "I'm still looking forward to them. I'm not going to miss my chance with Burt Reynolds."

Burt read the comments with amusement. Dolly is a devoted wife despite her frequent separations from her husband because of the demands of her career. Burt was glad of the opportunity to play opposite her, and prepared for the romance rumors that were sure to circulate.

In truth, he was very unhappy about the breakup with Sally, though he did stay in touch, especially with the kids.

"I love them [Peter and Eli]. I love them now as I loved them then. I think they are extraordinary children. They are just really unique human beings, but so is Sally.

"It's been a triple loss instead of a single loss, although I do get together with the kids, to play tennis or basketball with them."

He added thoughtfully, "In the past, whenever a relationship would go bad, I would try to figure out what the *other* person had done wrong. But, in this situation with Sally, I've been trying to figure out what *I've* done wrong. It's the first time I've ever done that. So maybe I'm growing up.

"If I ever have a chance with her again, I'm not going to blow it."

He had tried to get across to Sally the fact that he was over his anger and hurt. In part he blamed their separation on the media and those who twisted the facts regarding the Oscar situation. Slowly, they began to mend the break, and tentatively, treading very carefully along the way, they began to see each other again. But, though Sally still visited Burt on occasional weekends and he had clearly and publicly indicated his deep feelings for her, the relationship remained tenuous.

"I want to be her best friend," Burt said. "I miss her—and I'm sorry."

For the time being, Burt was forced to set his disappointment in love aside and concentrate instead on his career.

In preparation for the role in *The Best Little Whorehouse in Texas,* in which he has a solo number and sings a duet with Miss Parton, he began studying singing (with a cantor) and dancing. Filming on *Paternity* had closed down because of the actors' strike in the summer and fall of 1980, and Burt, unable to just sit around, devoted his time to the dinner theater.

"I enjoy juggling several balls at one time. I like starting the day that way. This morning I had a call with a panicky announcement that they couldn't find an actor to play the lead in *Harvey.* I calmed them down and took care of it myself. The dinner theater is a nice little place to do something. The audiences are really wonderful, and it lets me give something back to the community I came from."

It also provided an outlet for his energetic personality.

"Burt's just like what I thought he would be, a happy-go-lucky kind of guy. Very nice and smooth. He's steady," a teenage actor remarked.

Boy, girl, man, woman—it doesn't matter what the sex or age. There is something universal about the appeal of this outspoken, hard-working, caring man. It is the core of his appeal, the charisma that has endeared him to millions.

In August 1980, the National Association of Theater Owners again voted Burt Star of the Year. It is only the second time in the long history of the award that this honor has been bestowed to the same person in two successive years.

That same month, the reviews of the newly released *Smokey and the Bandit 2* termed it a clone of the first *Smokey.* But, the first weekend of its release, the film earned $1,000,000.

"I have a tendency to rotate between really giving a damn about *everything* and not giving a damn about *anything.* As I get older, I'm starting to settle into the middle of those feelings. I realize that to keep your sanity, you have to give a damn only about your work and the people that you love. I may fight it at times, but I've gotten to the point where I know I have to take those risks that are necessary when you are vulnerable. And you have to not give a damn about anything else."

On a Barbara Walters television interview he joked about his days as a young actor. "I was a combination of Marlon Brando and Yvonne de Carlo."

"I don't play around," he had said in a magazine interview. "When I'm involved with one woman, I'm involved with one woman, period. But, between romances, I'm carnivorous."

He had also admitted once that for a long time after his breakup with Dinah, he had been virtually celibate. As the romance with Sally hit a dead end, there seemed to be no one new on the horizon. Burt's love life appeared to be in cold storage. It was not in keeping with his "macho" image. But it is certainly in keeping with who and what he really is, according to those who are privy to this side of him.

He was launching another important project—producing, directing, and starring in *Sharky's Machine*. The close of 1980 found him revving up for it.

But, more than his work, he was basking in the knowledge that his public adored, approved of, and accepted him. A *World Almanac* survey of junior high school students had placed him at the top of the list of "Famous or Important Living Persons You Most Admire."

CHAPTER
EIGHTEEN

lthough he had not been able to fulfill his desire to complete the two years he needed for his college degree, Burt had not been forgotten by his former school.

January 14, 1981, was one of the most touching days of his life. Dressed in cap and gown, he received an honorary Doctorate of Humane Letters from FSU.

A beaming Dean Richard Fallon praised Reynolds for "giving of the most valuable things he has—his time and talent—not just his money."

In conclusion, Dean Fallon said, "This degree, ladies and gentlemen, has been earned."

In an editorial that appeared in an FSU publication, editor James P. Jones wrote, "Burt Reynolds has given Florida State University something even more important—his love."

"I have a reputation for being irreverent," Burt said, standing tall before the crowd who had gathered to witness the ceremony. "I am not irreverent about this. I thank you. I thank God and I will love this university for the rest of my life and will try to make you proud of me."

The honorary doctorate bestowed upon Burt that day was the sixtieth in the 123-year history of the university. Afterwards, Burt had to plunge through the throngs of autograph seekers who had gathered outside the fine arts building on the university campus. And, as usual, he stopped to oblige eager fans, kidding with them in his easy, friendly manner.

"The only bad thing about being famous, for me personally, is the fact that I am a big people-watcher. I could do it for hours on end. But it's difficult to watch people when they're looking at you," he once admitted. Nevertheless, he has always been patient and kind to those adoring fans who seem to dog his every footstep.

Later, Dean Fallon was to comment with obvious emotion, "We love him. We love this man."

In Atlanta, where he appeared with Sammy Davis, Jr., and Frank Sinatra in a benefit concert to raise funds for further investigation of the spate of mysterious murders of several black children, Burt added $10,000 of his own money to the $148,000 raised at the concert.

A few months later it was announced that the New York Friars Club had selected him as their Man of the Year. The event that took place in the Waldorf Astoria was held on May 16—a memorable evening in which friends from show biz and his childhood as well as members of his family joined in to honor him at a black-tie dinner that cost $750 a plate.

When Dinah Shore sang a love song, her face glowing with tender affection, her eyes focused on him, there were more than a few audible sighs in the ballroom packed with people.

"When the history of this particular age is recorded," she remarked afterwards, "it will be in the books that Burt Reynolds has done more for little old ladies in tennis shoes than anyone." With that, she deftly lifted the hem of her gown to reveal the sneakers she wore. It brought the house down.

"I don't know about little old ladies," Burt retorted, "but you knock my socks off."

After much kidding and a few sentiments expressed by those friends who had been chosen to verbalize the reason for honoring him, Burt was presented with the traditional Friars statuette and a gold Corum watch.

"I'll probably never win an Oscar, so I'll do my speech now," Burt quipped. "I may not be Brando or Pacino, but, dammit, I do show up [at award dinners]. I invited everyone here that I love.

"I'll make you proud of me. I've got something real good in

me and it's going to pop out one day and all those people out there will be surprised. Except for you here tonight."

Burt's parents and his sister and brother beamed proudly as Burt directed his heartfelt promise to them.

The evening rang with humor as speakers kidded Burt about his macho image. But along with the funny cracks were expressions of admiration for Burt's continuous generosity.

At the close of the roast, Burt solemnly requested that everyone stand up, and, directing them with the fine touch that has made him so popular, he asked that they repeat with him, "We have to love each other." It is his creed, one that he tries very hard to live by on a daily basis.

Sally, on location filming, had not been able to make the party. She sent a wire of congratulations and, friends said, a personal note just for Burt to read.

Another friend who was unable to make the ceremony due to another engagement had also wired his good wishes. It was signed Ronald Reagan.

"I thought I was rich when I signed an acting contract for three hundred seventy-five dollars a week," Burt once commented. "I never think about wealth. What does jolt me is when I'm reading a book and someone tells me the President is on the phone." The telegram from the President and Nancy no doubt had the same effect.

Always on the lookout for property, Burt purchased acreage in Hana, the noncommercial area of Maui in the Hawaiian Islands. Carol Burnett, with whom he has a close friendship, recently moved there, and it seemed that Burt was planning to build a home on the island as well.

During the time that Burt had been deep in his sorrow at losing Sally, Hal Needham had been falling in love. In late June, riding on horseback alongside the groom, Burt was best man at an unusual wedding that took place before a crowd of six hundred cheering "pals" on a studio backlot in a western "church." The bride was driven up to the church in a carriage. An unusual, highly theatrical, but certainly memorable wedding.

Burt flew back to Hollywood from location on *Sharky's Machine* to be immortalized in cement in September. As the 160th personality to have his foot- and handprints inscribed in concrete in the forecourt of the former Grauman's Chinese Theatre, Burt paused to remember how it once had been. "I used to come here when I first came to town. I would put my feet in Doug Fairbanks' print and I'd think what small feet he had. Just think, someday someone might be saying that about me."

Alongside the handprints and the impression of a pair of square-toed cowboy boots, he wrote, "To the public that made this all possible. Love Ya. Burt Reynolds."

Sometime that fall, a guest on the "A.M. Los Angeles" show remarked to co-hostess (former Miss America) Tawny Little that Burt wanted to meet her, and that he thought she was very nice and very pretty. Tawny, who is also an ABC newscaster, seemed taken aback but pleased.

Soon after that, the two began appearing together socially, and from time to time, Tawny's co-host, Paul Moyer, would make sly references to the fact that they were an item.

The glamorous newscaster commented that it was fair to say that their dating had been going on for a couple of months, and she was seeing Burt often. "I've dated him a little, but that doesn't mean we're having an affair."

But it was also rumored that Sally and Burt were still trying to work out their problems. For fans eager to read more about Burt's romantic life, it was very confusing.

For Burt and Sally it was even more so.

While Burt prepared for *The Best Little Whorehouse in Texas,* he also attended to the completion of another plan that had long been on his agenda. He has signed with the Fondas—Jane and Peter—to join Marlon Brando in a TV mini-series of *Bury My Heart at Wounded Knee,* to be filmed in Seattle. While the date had not been set, Burt was very excited about the project. It's a subject about which he has always felt strongly.

But in November he received yet another show-business honor. The Variety Clubs International "All-Star Party for Burt Reynolds" was taped in a studio in Burbank, and aired on CBS in December. It was a very special salute to a very special member of the entertainment world. On hand to pay him tribute were Dom DeLuise, Anne Murray, Dolly Parton, and James Stewart.

"I can't speak for others in my profession who have been as fortunate as I have been, but I never tire of winning recognition," Burt said. "Each one catches me off-guard and I greet it with a kind of 'are you sure you mean me?' reaction.

"Each one is special."

Frank Sinatra said of him, "In honoring Burt Reynolds, we pay tribute to Everyman. Burt's that kind of a guy. He's the one ladies like to dance with, their husbands like to drink with. He is the larger-than-life actor of our times. Gifted, talented, naughty and nice."

James Stewart, seated near Burt's parents, remarked, "Your son is doing real well in the picture business."

The senior Reynolds, as always, beamed with love and pride. Their boy has done all right for himself.

That Christmas was especially nice. Perhaps he felt a twinge of loneliness, of missing Sally. But the year had been one of great satisfaction. The reviews of his latest films had been encouraging as well.

Of *Rough Cut* they had said: ". . . Reynolds has a proven way with comedy." Of *Paternity:* ". . . Reynolds is the mainstay of the piece. *Paternity* plays for soft laughs."

The new year began on a low note for Burt. While resting up on the ranch before starting his new picture *Best Friends,* in which he co-stars with Goldie Hawn, he underwent surgery for a recurrent hernia. It was the same condition that had caused him so much discomfort in 1973.

But by February 11, his forty-sixth birthday, Burt was feeling well enough to put in an appearance on "The Tonight Show," where host Johnny Carson had prepared a little birthday celebration.

No one laughed louder than Burt when a larger-than-life photo of him was revealed and Johnny went through a brief "This Is Your Life" flashback. As the cake was wheeled out, candles lit, the expression on Burt's face was clearly one of affection . . . for his good friend on stage, for those wonderful people in the audience cheering and shouting *Happy Birthday.*

Johnny and Burt spent a while just joshing around in their usual easy manner, good friends throwing harmless barbs at one another. The audience ate it up, as always.

As Burt blew out the candles, we wondered what he might have wished for. One can perhaps make an attempt to guess.

Years ago he commented that he hoped to be settled down,

128

married with kids by the time he is fifty. Producer Dick McInnes recalls a conversation with Burt before air time on a local talk show. "I was telling Burt about my daughter, and he said 'I really envy you.' Imagine Burt Reynolds envying *me.*"

Wishes are the stuff that dreams are made of, and there are two wishes very close to Burt's heart that have not yet come true. Perhaps as he blew out the candles on his birthday cake before millions of television viewers Burt was thinking of the relationship with actress Loni Anderson that had just begun to develop, wishing that this time would be the charm. This time maybe that wish for marriage and family, which he has always wanted, would come true. Perhaps that was his wish.

But there is still another fantasy that, were it to come true right now, would perhaps mean even more to him: to win an Oscar.

Rex Reed once said to him, "You know, the critics have never been able to hurt you [at the box office]. That's probably what gets us so angry." Still, the dream of an Academy Award persists.

Burt Reynolds is the kind of person who will hold fast to his dream until it comes true.

Robert Beverly Ray wrote of Burt in *The Wall Street Journal,* "He's the perfect movie star."

This, the essence of Burt Reynolds, has kept him at the top for more than a decade. To be the perfect movie star and yet be a part of the mainstream is a neat trick.

It is one that Mr. Reynolds has mastered with what appears to be no effort at all.

Index

132